C000319086

ALL ABOUT YOUR PONY

GEORGIE HENSCHEL

WARD LOCK

© George Henschel 1981, 1989

This edition first published in Great Britain in 1989
by Ward Lock Limited, Artillery House,
Artillery Row, London SW1P 1RT,
a Cassell Company
Reprinted 1989

Previously published as
'A Horseman's Handbook'

Layout by Charlotte Westbrook
House editor Suzanna Osman Jones

Cover photography by Bob Langrish

Text set in 10/12pt Times
by Graphicraft Typesetters, Hong Kong

Printed in Great Britain by
Hollen Street Press Ltd, Slough

British Library Cataloguing in Publication Data

Henschel, Georgie
  All about your pony. – (*Ward Lock's Riding School*)
  1. Ponies – Juvenile literature
  I. Title   II. Series
  636.1'6   SF315

ISBN 0-7063-6785-5

Contents

DEDICATION

To my ponies, in gratitude.

Acknowledgements

Colour photographs: Kit Houghton pages 78 and 79; Leslie Lane page 33 below; Bob Langrish page 52; Peter Roberts pages 34 and 51; Sally Anne Thompson/Animal Photography page 80; Zefa pages 52 and 77. *Black and white photographs:* British Tourist Authority page 98; John Corsan page 63; John Elliott pages 17, 22, 23 and 24; Eventer/Peter Doresa page 38; Candida Geddes pages 1, 8, 18, 29, 36, 39, 40, 44, 55, 57, 60, 67, 70, 75 and 83; Sarah King page 86; Leslie Lane pages 13, 15, 20 above and centre, 64 and 84; A.C. Littlejohns page 96; Jane Miller page 6; Sally Anne Thompson/Animal Photography page 20 below; John Topham pages 54 and 90.

We hope that any suppliers of photographs inadvertently omitted from this list will accept a general acknowledgement.

Line drawings: Christine Bousfield.

1 Understanding ponies

All animals, ourselves included, are either carnivores, that is, meat eaters; or herbivores, that is, vegetarians, living on grass and herbage.

Horses and ponies are herbivores. Carnivores are the hunters; herbivores, the hunted, or the preyed upon.

They are also gregarious: which means they like the company of their own kind. In the wild they live in herds, which gives them a feeling of security. Although herd leaders will fight to defend the herd, they are not natural fighters; their instinct is to avoid or run away from danger. Because hunted animals in the wild have always to be ready to run from danger, their young are born with the full use of their legs, able to keep up with the herd a few hours after birth. At liberty, grazing animals are eating small amounts almost all the time. They have relatively small stomachs, and their digestive systems require small quantities of food passed through from the stomach fairly constantly.

Obviously, these two groups of animals, the hunters and the hunted, have quite different instincts, different natural ways of reacting to outside happenings, and to ourselves. It is important to know something about these instincts, because the three most familiar domestic animals, dogs, cats, and horses and ponies, belong to different groups, dogs and cats being hunters. Horses and ponies, however domesticated and well-trained, still have many of the instincts of the wild, hunted animals from which they descend, instincts which make them suspicious of anything strange, and want to run away from what frightens or startles them. They are more highly strung than hunter-group animals are, and that includes ourselves! All their senses are constantly alert to possible danger.

In domesticating horses and ponies, we have taken them away from the herd, where they felt secure and protected. It is up to us to let them

This little Welsh Pony mare is licking her newly born foal to dry it, and help to warm its body. Foals, when they first come into the world, are damp and very soon feel cold if they are not dried and warmed by their mothers licking them. Nearly all mares do this instinctively. If some young mares do not, then humans have to help the foal by rubbing it dry with a soft towel. This little foal hasn't been long on its legs; you can see by the way it has splayed out its hind legs that it is finding it difficult to keep its balance.

feel equally secure in our care. We must give them confidence, whether handling, training, riding or just talking to them in the field. Those that have complete confidence in the people who ride or handle them will do all sorts of things which instinct would make them fear: they will go calmly through heavy traffic, walk into trailers, or up the steep ramps of lorries, and will let themselves be driven about in blinkers. They will jump obstacles which they'd never think of tackling on their own. They have learnt that if their riders are not frightened, there is no reason for them to be; that if they're asked to walk into small or large boxes on wheels, there are not going to be lions or wolves waiting for them inside!

As for jumping, if their riders believe they can get over an obstacle, then it must be true. Unfortunately for the willing horse or pony, this isn't always so. Ambitious riders can 'over face' their mounts: that is, ask them to jump things they know are really too big and difficult. This is not only unkind, but silly. It will lead to the horse or pony losing confidence both in its rider and its own ability to jump, and may end by putting it off jumping altogether.

Once horses and ponies have confidence in us, they trust us, and submit to our demands, as they would their herd leader in the wild. Treat them badly, or even wrongly, and they lose that confidence, become insecure, and can end up by becoming 'problems'. Very few are born vicious, or what are called 'rogues'; they have been made so by wrong, rough, or cruel handling. The horse is not aggressive by nature, but if it is badly treated, bullied into submission or knocked about in its box in a misguided effort to 'teach it manners', it can't escape by running away, so its natural reaction is to defend itself with teeth and heels. Only people with patience and understanding can give back confidence in humans to this kind of spoiled horse. But horses have long memories; they will always remember their tormentors; if they see them again they will show their teeth and heels.

Making friends with ponies

If we like ponies, it's natural to want to be with them: to handle them, touch them, pat them; whether they're our own, or at a riding school, or just ponies in a nearby field. It's also natural to want them to like, accept, and have confidence in us. If we're sensible, this isn't hard.

Ponies, by nature, are more easily startled than dogs or cats. You can pat your sleeping dog and get only a tailwag as a response, but if you suddenly slap your pony on the backside while it is eating, it's

7

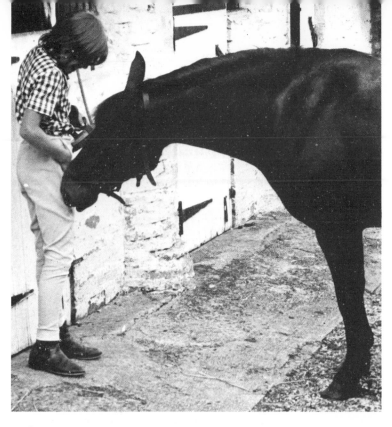

Ponies very soon get to know which pocket you are hiding some titbits in! Provided your pony only nuzzles for his treat and doesn't try to nip you, and that you don't give him a titbit EVERY time you talk to him, there is nothing against letting him know that if he is good, he can expect a 'goody'!

your own fault if it kicks out at you. Never make sudden movements with a pony. If it is stabled, speak to it before you open the door. It may be resting, asleep or half-asleep; burst in suddenly and it will back away in fright.

If you want to catch your pony in the field, walk slowly towards it, calling to it. If you rush up, bridle in hand, it will rush away, rather faster. If it is a new pony, or wary of being caught, take a bowl or bucket with a little food in it; call to attract the pony's attention, show it the food bucket, and stand still. It will come to you; then let it eat a little before you put on its halter. But if ponies are fed every time they are caught and brought in, most will soon start coming to the gate when you call them.

If you just want to talk to ponies in a field, call to them; then stand still at the gate or the fence. Curiosity will bring them over to have a look at you. Never go into a field of ponies with titbits in your pocket. They will know you have them; jealousy and in-fighting will result, and you may be caught uncomfortably in the middle. Titbits should only be given as rewards, such as at the end of a lesson. Ponies quickly acquire the habit of nuzzling and later nipping you or your clothes, looking for titbits. Then, because nipping shouldn't be tolerated you have to give them a smack, which confuses them. Why be allowed to nuzzle for titbits one day, and smacked for doing so the next? Don't let them get into the habit of expecting titbits, and never give them to a pony without asking the owner.

We don't have to bribe ponies to like us, and to like being petted and talked to. They like the sound of our voices and become quick to recognize the different ways we can speak to them: quietly and soothingly when we are pleased with them; firmly when we want them to do something particular, like move over in the stable, and crossly if they have been naughty, when we have to say 'NO' very firmly indeed. Never shout; ponies' hearing is far more acute than ours, shouting sounds so loud it only frightens them, they become confused and lose confidence in us.

Ponies, like dogs, can learn the meaning of quite a number of words if the same ones are always used for the same thing, and spoken in the same tone of voice. The obvious ones are 'walk on', 'trot' – a very easy one for them to learn because of its sharp sound – and 'whoa', or 'halt'. But there are lots of others. For instance, when you want your pony to lift its feet for you to clean them, if you say 'lift', as you run your hand down its legs, you'll find that one day, to your surprise, all you have to do is say 'lift' for it to give you its foot.

Every kind of animal has its own kind of intelligence; like ourselves, some individuals will always have more than others. The better we understand how to handle and talk to ponies so that they understand us, the more the intelligence of each one will develop; but it will always be a different intelligence from our own. We should never make the mistake of giving animals human characters, or qualities. Many animals have rather nicer characters than many humans, and all have more sensitive reactions to the natural world around them.

On the other hand, we shouldn't think that because ponies are 'just animals', they have no feelings or emotions. They have. We have learnt that because their ancestors were hunted animals, they react strongly to fear. Against that, if they are secure and contented in their surroundings and confident in their riders, they can be incredibly bold. They can be bored, and they can be excited and interested, they have long memories for places, people and each other just as we do. They can probably feel something like resentment against people who have ill-treated them. Nor do they forget people whom they have liked; they often recognize them again after years of separation. They do not show their affection noisily as dogs do, but by a soft nicker of welcome, and being calm and trustful. If you go into the loose box of a resting pony, and instead of jumping to its feet it stays quietly lying down, it shows that it has complete confidence in you. By domesticating ponies we have made them entirely dependent on us, so they can feel desperately lonely if we neglect them, or in their old age turn them out alone, or send them on long frightening journeys to sales or slaughter-houses.

To be friends with all ponies, you should never forget their pony natures, inherited from the past. Approach quietly, don't rush at them waving your arms about, or make sudden movements. Handle them calmly but firmly; never shout or lose your temper. Talk to them, pat them, become fond of them but don't get so sentimental that you let them get away with all sorts of naughtinesses. Be consistent in the way you treat them so they know what is expected of them. They'll only become confused if you encourage them to do something one day, and the next are cross with them for doing it. However much you like ponies, it's just as important that they should like you, which they will do if they have the same confidence in you as, in the wild, they would have had in their herd leader.

Never tease ponies. Humans are the only animals which can cope with being teased, and we don't always enjoy it!

2 Pony breeds

If you live in the British Isles, you are lucky to have so many different breeds of native ponies, that is, ponies which have lived and bred in particular parts of England, Scotland, Wales and Ireland, for a very long time. Because once upon a time these ponies lived wild, and had to forage for themselves and keep themselves warm in winter, they are all tough and hardy, strong for their size, and grow thick coats in winter as protection from the weather.

There are nine of these native breeds, of which the overall family name is 'Mountain and Moorland' ponies. So when you see in a show schedule, classes for 'Mountain and Moorland Ponies', it is for ponies of one or sometimes all of the nine native breeds. For a long time each breed lived, bred, and later was used by man in its own particular district. Each is still distinct and different. They range in height from the tiny Shetland, which must not be more than 42 inches (106.7 cm); to the Dales, Connemaras and Highlands, which often measure the full pony height of 14.2 hh, or 14 hands 2 inches high; 'hh' means hands high, and a hand measures 4 inches (10 cm).

There is therefore a native pony to suit all riders, from six to sixty years. They are fun to own and look after because they are full of character, game, and safe to ride because they are clever and sure-footed over rough country. All the native breeds can live out of doors happily all year round, provided they have some shelter, natural or a shed, in their field, and in winter, enough to eat to keep them warm and healthy. We shall discover in Chapter 3 that they do not need quite so much food, weight for height, as ponies with only a little native blood, so they are less expensive to keep.

In the past, the native ponies of each breed were used for many purposes by people in their districts, so they are all versatile: that is, they can be good at more than one kind of work.

Let's see what these native breeds are: what they look like, and for what each is most suitable.

11

1 Shetland
2 Highland
3 Fell
4 Dales
5 Connemara
6 Welsh
7 Exmoor
8 New Forest
9 Dartmoor

This map shows you the parts of the British Isles from which the different breeds of native ponies originate. Most are also bred in lots of other districts now, and some abroad; but the map shows where their natural homes are. Each breed has its own Society, which keeps a register of all pedigree ponies, and of the studs which breed them.

The Shetland Pony

Starting with the smallest, the Shetland; the original home of these ponies is the Shetland Islands, off the north coast of Scotland. Until the coming of the car and tractor ponies were the work horses of the islands. They helped the crofter and small farmer cultivate his land; as

12

Shetland Pony.

Dartmoor Pony.

Exmoor Pony.

pack ponies, they brought peat, the islanders' only fuel, down from the moors, and they were used as transport, both ridden and driven. Of all equines, they are probably the strongest in relation to their tiny height. A great many Shetlands were pit ponies in coal mines, some being bred specially for this.

Today, Shetlands are bred all over Britain, and in many other countries. The pity is that many people forget, or do not know about, their varied and very active past, they tend to treat them as pets and then, because the ponies haven't enough to do they become bored and spoilt. If they are properly handled and broken, kept in work and not allowed to get too fat, Shetlands can be as active and useful as any other pony breed. They can make excellent first ponies; many jump well. A Shetland has won the small height division of Working Hunter Pony classes (see page 85); and they go very well in harness. Shetlands are measured in inches: the height limit is 42 inches (106.7 cm) for a stallion; the average is between 38 and 40 inches (96.5–101.6 cm). Shetlands are found in all colours.

All the other bigger breeds are measured in hands (see above); 'hh' is the abbreviation for hands high.

The next breeds in height are the *Dartmoor,* the *Exmoor,* and the *Welsh Mountain,* the limit for all three being 12.2 hh.

The Dartmoor Pony
Dartmoors are super riding ponies; very active but with easy co-operative temperaments. They are very strong for their size; in their native home, the West of England, they are often ridden by adults, but they have kind temperaments and so are very suitable for children. They are usually brown, bay or black.

The Exmoor Pony
The Exmoor is the oldest of all the native breeds. Its existence was recorded in 1085 in a survey of England called The Domesday Book; but it is much older than that. It has some characteristics of conformation found in the fossilized remains of prehistoric ponies, not found in any other contemporary breed. Exmoor ponies always have light oatmealy-coloured markings round their muzzles, their eyes, and under their bellies: these are called 'mealy markings'. They have specially dense, springy coats, and distinctive tails, with a spreading, fan-like growth at the top. Like the Dartmoor, they are strong for their size, capable if necessary of carrying adults. They are

Welsh Pony Section B.

Connemara Pony.

Fell Pony.

self-reliant and exceptionally intelligent. A book about an Exmoor pony called 'Moorland Mousie' will tell you a lot about this breed. Exmoor ponies are brown, bay, and sometimes a mousy-dun colour.

The Welsh Pony

Although in the total of nine Mountain and Moorland breeds the Welsh are counted as only one, there are in fact four types of Welsh Ponies. These are labelled Sections A, B, C, and D, and are divided according to size. Welsh Ponies can be any colour except piebald or skewbald.

Section A – Welsh Mountain Pony

The Welsh Mountain, the smallest Welsh section, is the most beautiful of the native breeds, and is also very ancient. When Julius Caesar was in Britain, he founded a stud of these ponies in Merionethshire and introduced some Eastern, probably Arabian, horses to interbreed with the native stock. Many Welsh Mountains today have the dished profile, the large, intelligent, wide-set eyes and the proud bearing typical of the Arabian. They are kind and gentle, but courageous and with their fair share of what the Welsh call 'hwyl'; which can be translated as verve, or fire. They are therefore better ponies for competent young riders than for beginners. But they are not only beautiful. They are strong, tough, and hardy, capable of living out in winter in all weathers, and winning in the show ring and competing in Pony Club events in the summer.

Section B – Welsh Pony

Section B ponies are bigger; their height limit is 13.2 hh. Though the type is based on the Welsh Mountain, Thoroughbred and Arab blood has been used to increase height. Section B's are the riding ponies of Wales; at many shows, they can be shown in both Welsh and the Riding Pony classes. Good Section B's, however, should still be recognizably Welsh, with fine pony heads and all the sturdiness of the Mountain ponies, but with the extra scope and lower action given to them by their increased height. (See page 6).

Welsh Mountain Ponies, the smallest of the Welsh, are very versatile. As well as being super riding ponies, they are often driven. Here is a pair being driven tandem (that is, one in front of the other) in a Combined Driving Event. In a tandem, the front horse is called the leader, the one nearest the vehicle, the wheeler.

Section C – Welsh Pony of Cob Type

Section C ponies run to the same height as the B's but are chunkier and stronger. They are also based on the Mountain pony but quite a lot of different blood has gone into the establishment of this type, including Hackney, and an older breed of trotting horse called the Norfolk Roadster. They are smaller editions of the big Welsh Cob; very strong, courageous, hardy and intelligent. Because they are quite up to carrying an adult rider, they are suitable for children at school, as parents can also ride and keep them exercised in term time. Having a super trot, they go well in harness. While the A's and the B's are bred all over Britain, and in many other countries, the C's are still mostly bred in Wales, many of the best with names carrying the prefix 'Symod'.

Each of these three small Welsh breeds is often used as 'foundation stock': that is, to cross with Thoroughbreds or Arabs to produce Riding Ponies or quality small horses. A 'Riding Pony' is a more elegant, refined creature than a native pony, with good conformation and extra quality but retaining pony character.

Section D – Welsh Cobs

Section D animals are the big Welsh Cobs, which are not always ponies as they run from 14.2 hh to 15.2 hh. If there is no special class for Welsh Cobs at a show they can be shown, ridden or in-hand, in the class for 'Mountain and Moorland, Large Breeds'. (See page 24).

The Fell Pony

This is an old breed with an interesting history. When the Romans were in Britain, they imported about a thousand black Friesian horses into the North of England from Holland, mostly stallions, to cross with and improve the quality of local native ponies. Those horses are the remote ancestors of the Fell Pony of today, which although smaller is similar in type to the Friesian Horse. Also, although Fell ponies can be brown or bay, the majority, like the Friesians, are black, with no white markings.

In the past they were the all-purpose ponies of the people who lived in Cumberland and Westmoreland. They worked the land; as pack ponies, they carried lead from the mines to cities and ports, and when there was no work to be done, they took part in trotting races. Like their ancestors, the Friesians, they are fast trotters. Fells are very hardy and easy to keep. Many trekking centres use them because they are so sensible, and sure-footed across rough country. A Fell Pony should not be higher than 14 hands.

Now for the four breeds that are allowed to go up to 14.2 hh in the breed regulations.

The Connemara Pony
This breed comes from Ireland, although it is now bred in many other countries. Many of these ponies are natural jumpers; they can perform well in every kind of activity and although very active and courageous, are also gentle and easy to handle. The biggest ones are quite up to adults' weight. A great many Connemaras today are grey. But there is a rich, slightly mottled golden dun colour, with black mane and tail and black points which is very typical. Although they can be as small as 13 hh, and as high as 14.2 hh, most are around 14 hh. (See page 78).

The New Forest Pony
Herds of ponies have run in the New Forest, in the South of England, for a very long time. During that long time, however, stallions of so many different breeds have been turned out to run with the mares that it has not been easy for serious breeders of New Forest Ponies to establish a type. Although ponies do still run in the Forest, owned by people who have what are called 'commoners' grazing rights, the best are bred in private studs. And the best are very good indeed, being real 'family ponies', capable of carrying parents as well as children, docile, easy to handle, sure-footed and going well in harness, too. They are very popular abroad. New Forest ponies have been exported to more foreign countries than probably any other native breed. Like the Welsh, they can be any colour except piebald and skewbald.

The Dales Pony
These ponies, like the Fells, come from the North of England, but from the eastern counties of Northumberland, Durham and parts of Yorkshire. Their remote ancestors were probably the same kind of mares from which the Fells, crossed with the black horses from Holland, originated. But while Fell breeders have always been against introducing outside blood, Dales ponies owe a lot to the Welsh Cob, in particular, to one stallion called Comet.

19

New Forest Pony.

Dales Pony.

Icelandic Pony.

Comet lived about 100 years ago and served a lot of Dales mares, some of whom may have had some carthorse blood. The result is that the Dales pony, although big and heavily built, has inherited from Comet the Welsh Cob's superb vitality, and fast, free and straight-actioned trot. At one time, like the Fells, they were used as pack ponies to carry lead from the mines to the docks, many of them carrying loads of 100 kg (16 stone) 65 km (40 miles) in a day. Crossed with Thoroughbreds, Dales ponies can produce all-round, competitive riding horses. They are usually black or dark brown, and sometimes grey.

The Highland Pony
These ponies, because of their good natures and their sure-footedness, are used a lot for trekking, a holiday pastime that originated in Scotland. But they are much more versatile than is generally recognized. As they can vary in height from 13 hh to 14.2 hh, there are Highlands to suit all ages and sizes of rider, although even the smaller ones are able to carry adults. In the past, they were used as all-purpose ponies on crofts and small farms; working the land, going in harness and often ridden by shepherds going their rounds. They were also used as 'deer ponies' and many still are: bringing, slung over their backs, the deer shot by stalkers down from the hills. These activities tended to make people forget their riding potential, which, when they are properly broken, schooled, and fed, is as good as that of the two other heavy breeds, the Fell and the Dales.

They are intelligent, active and willing and many jump well enough to take part in Riding and Pony Club activities and to be clever, safe hunters. Their most usual colours are grey, and all shades of dun, from a dark elephant grey called 'mouse dun', to a rich golden dun with dark points. Black, brown and bay are old colours, but not seen often today. Nearly all have an eel stripe: a dark line along their backs; and many have zebra markings: horizontal dark stripes on the back of their forelegs. (See pages 33 and 79).

Other countries have their own breeds of native pony. There are three breeds to be seen quite often in Britain: the Icelandic, the Norwegian Fjord, and the Austrian Haflinger. Icelandic ponies are small, but very strong; like Shetlands on the islands, they were for centuries the only work animals in Iceland, and the only means of transport. They have a distinctive gait called the 'tolt', which is a

This picture shows the Hon. Mrs Kidd driving a pair of Norwegian Fjord Ponies at the Royal Windsor show. Mrs Kidd has been very successful with her Norwegians, and has a stud of them. Notice that the ponies' manes are hogged, which is the way they are always turned out in Norway. Driving events are becoming very popular, and 'Combined Driving' is exciting to watch, as it includes dressage and turnout; a cross country drive, with a number of hazards, one of which is always through water; and an obstacle section.

lateral trot; the legs moving in pairs on the same side, not diagonally.

Norwegian Fjord ponies are always cream dun, with an eel stripe, and two-coloured manes (which stand up) and tails: dark in the centre, cream to the sides. They are charming ponies, very easy to handle, comfortable to ride, and go very well in harness. A pair of

Norwegian ponies is often seen competing in driving events. Norwegians are usually 13.2 hh to 14.2 hh. (See pages 77 and 78).

Haflingers are always a rich, bright chestnut, with lighter manes and tails. Like the Norwegians, they have very nice temperaments, and go as well in harness as they do under saddle. They are a little smaller than Norwegians, averaging just under 14 hh.

Each breed has its own Breed Society, which looks after its interests, and keeps records of all the ponies that have pedigrees, and whose owners have registered them with the society (see Societies and useful addresses).

Of course, there are lots of ponies without pedigrees, who may belong to a particular breed all the same, or who may be a mixture. If you know what the breeds look like, it can be interesting to try to

Haflinger Pony; this breed is Austrian.

The biggest Welsh, the Cobs, are also versatile; they have a fast and spectacular trot. Here is a Welsh Cob being driven at the Royal Welsh Show. Welsh Cobs have been very successful in Combined Driving competitions; they also cross well with Thoroughbreds.

work out which one a pony most resembles. Naturally, registered ponies of any breed are usually more expensive than ponies without pedigrees. That doesn't necessarily mean that they are better, or nicer, ponies. For a pony of your own, it's far more important that you should like each other and get on well than that the pony should have a long line of distinguished ancestors!

3 Pony care and feeding

'Care' is a funny word, with more than one meaning. To take care of something, or someone, is to look after it, and see it comes to no harm.

To care *for* something means that you like it; and feel affection for it. Caring for ponies then, means more than just looking after them. It means that you care for the ponies that are in your charge but you can care for ponies a lot and not own one. If you don't own one, you may be lucky enough to be having riding lessons. Obviously, you are not taking care of the pony; the riding school is doing that; but you should care for the pony you are learning on, rather than think of it as a sort of four-legged bicycle.

Or perhaps you have a friend with a pony you help to look after. You will then find it useful to know something about feeding; what sort of things ponies eat, and how much. So let's discover what ponies should eat.

Basic feeding rules
Although ponies at liberty are eating a little almost constantly obviously they can't when we want to ride them. Yet their digestions are organized to cope with that way of eating. How do we feed our working ponies so that they don't get stomach upsets, which we call 'colic'? – by following as closely as we can the three generally accepted basic rules of feeding. These are:

1 Feed little and often.
2 Do not work your pony hard after a full meal, when it has a full stomach.
3 Water before feeding.

'FEED LITTLE AND OFTEN' applies specially to the energy or concentrate feeds which working ponies need. So we must understand the difference between concentrate feeds, and the type of food ponies eat for the rest of the time: grass and hay, called 'bulk' food.

Ponies that are not working can live on good grass or hay alone. They are using no extra energy, so this will give them enough nourishment to keep them well covered, and warm. When we ask them to work they are going to use extra energy, which must be replaced if we don't want them to lose condition, or become tired. So we give them some concentrate food, containing protein, starch, sugar and vitamins.

Concentrate food

The amount of concentrate food will depend on the amount of work the pony is doing. Also, to some extent, on its individual character and temperament. Some ponies become too excitable on certain kinds of concentrates; others may need quite a lot if they are to work with energy and enthusiasm. The principal energy producing concentrates are: barley, pony cubes or coarse mixes. Oats are full of nourishment and easily digested. However, they can have a very exciting effect on some ponies so unless you are a very competent rider it is better to feed either cubes, or barley, which contains almost as much nourishment as oats, but is far less 'exciting'! Barley should be fed bruised or flaked, or, sometimes in winter, boiled, when you use it whole. You boil up the kernels, and when they've absorbed all the water, you mix them with bran.

There are many different brands of cubes; for ponies, buy the ordinary ones, not 'racehorse cubes', which will have a surprising effect on your pony, nor 'stud cubes', which are specially balanced for brood mares and young stock. The advantage of cubes is that they are always the same; whereas you can have good and bad quality oats or barley. There are also nowadays other patent feeds; 'Main Ring' is one. These should be fed according to the makers' instructions. You should never feed cubes, or 'cake', made for cattle. These have been specially prepared for ruminants (animals which chew the cud) and can be very damaging to horses and ponies.

Additional concentrate foods are: maize, which is a warming extra in winter; and sugar beet pulp, or cubes, which must be soaked before being fed. Sugar beet is very appetizing and helps to keep ponies in condition.

It is these concentrate feeds which must be given in small quantities. We've already learnt that horses and ponies have relatively small stomachs; 3 to 4 lbs (1.5–2 kg) is the most any pony's stomach can cope with at one meal. Therefore, if at any time you want your pony to have more concentrate food, you must give it an extra feed, not pile all the extra into one.

Bran is what remains of wheat after flour has been extracted from it by milling. It is an addition to feed rather than a food in itself. A little added to a feed prevents a pony from eating it too quickly. Feeds containing bran should be damped. It is also useful for making bran mashes. Better additions to concentrate feeds are forms of chaff, plain or molassed, such as Mollichaff or a Haymix.

Ponies can become very bored with exactly the same diet every day. If you decide to feed only cubes, or one of the patent food mixes, mix sometimes with damped bran, and now and then add a handful of barley or maize, soaked sugar beet, or sliced carrots.

'DO NOT WORK PONIES HARD AFTER A FULL MEAL'. This is important. Grass and hay they eat slowly. They eat appetizing concentrate feeds quickly, filling up their stomachs, which must be given time to begin passing the food through to their digestive systems. If ponies are worked before this starts happening, their stomachs, which are blown out like ours after a big meal, press on their lungs and make breathing difficult. It may also interfere with the stomach's normal process of passing the food on for slow digestion, and give the pony colic. You can go for a gentle hack half an hour or so after a feed; but before energetic work, ponies need at least an hour to digest in peace.

'WATER BEFORE FEEDING'. This is a rule that was more important in the days when ponies were led out to be watered, rather than having water constantly available, which it should be. It applies principally when coming back from a ride. Give the pony a chance to drink before giving it its feed. Ponies that can always drink when they want to will seldom be so thirsty that they drink too much at once. This is why it is important that stabled ponies should always have fresh clean water in their buckets, and in fields, there should be either running water, or water troughs kept clean and filled.

However much energy food our pony may need, it must have bulk food as well, to digest it. Bulk food is grass, and hay, which is dried grass.

Most ponies, certainly all 'native' breeds, can 'live out' happily all year round. It is better to say 'live out', than 'at grass' because it is only in spring, summer and early autumn that there is enough good in the grass to give them all the bulk they need. In most of the British Isles, there is little good in the grass in winter, even if it looks green, so ponies must have hay as well. On the other hand, when the grass comes fresh in spring, or if they're in a big field of good grass, they can easily eat *too much*. This will make them too fat and they may develop laminitis (see page 48). In spring and summer, if you want your pony to be able to do all the exciting things you want to, without puffing and blowing, it shouldn't be allowed to spend all its leisure time stuffing itself on grass.

When the grass is fresh and rich, it is a good idea to bring your pony in for at least part of every day. If you're at school, you may be able to persuade a parent or a friend to bring the pony in about midday if you can use a loose box or stable. It should have water, a small concentrate feed, and a small net of hay. If the pony can't be brought in, and it is in a big field, you could have an electric fence put up, and let it 'strip graze' the field; as dairy farmers do with cows. Most of us have plenty of time to look after our ponies at weekends, but it is unkind to leave them eating too much grass all week, and then at weekends, expect them to spend whole days galloping, jumping and going to gymkhanas.

How much to feed

Having discovered that all ponies need bulk food, and working ponies need energy food as well, let's see how much food in weight ponies of different heights and sizes should eat during 24 hours. The *maximum* weight a pony should have is discussed here; most native breeds do well on a little less than Riding Ponies of the same height, or those with Thoroughbred or Arab blood. This is because they have a different 'metabolism', which means the rate that the digestive process turns food into nourishment.

No one can lay down absolutely hard and fast rules for feeding because ponies are individuals, with their own needs, likes and dislikes, but this simple weight-for-height guide will be a help.

A pony of 14.2 hh should have not more than 24 lbs (11 kg) of food during a day and a night. Take away 1 lb (.45 kg) for every inch (2.5 cm) less of height. That makes 20 lbs (9 kg) for one of 13.2 hh; 16 lbs (7.25 kg) for one of 12.2 hh. In *winter* you should feed at least 14 lbs (6 kg) even to very small ponies, because the amount they need doesn't depend entirely on their height, but also on how much body surface there is exposed to the air, which has to be kept warm.

A sensible kind of water trough for a field, with no sharp edges. A self-filling trough is ideal, but will need scrubbing out regularly.

It's unkind to underfeed ponies; we can recognize those that look thin and miserable, but it's almost as unkind to overfeed them; to expect them to work when they're far too fat and heavy. So simple sums are necessary to feed neither too much nor too little.

We'll take the 14.2 hh pony as an example.

Let's say it is doing a lot of work: being ridden every day, sometimes on quite long rides; going to rallies and competitions and gymkhanas; and that it has a competent rider. It will need probably 9 lbs (4 kg) of concentrate food every day. Take 9 from 24, leaving 15; so it will need 15 lbs (6.75 kg) of bulk: grass or hay. If it is turned out at night, it will eat about 10 lbs (4.5 kg) of grass; if the grass is rich, a bit more. That leaves 5 lbs (2.25 kg) of hay, depending on the richness of the grass.

The principle is simple. Take away the weight of concentrate food from the total required weight of food, make up the total with bulk food. If the pony needs more concentrate food, give less bulk, so that the weight it is eating stays the same. If it is an excitable pony and needs less energy food, give it more bulk. It's quite easy to work out for ponies of different sizes. A 13 hh one, needing 18 lbs (8 kg), may be getting 6 lbs (2.75 kg) of energy food; then it needs 12 lbs (5.5 kg) of grass or hay, and so on.

It is the concentrates, the energy foods, which must be fed in small quantities. To go back to the 14.2 hh pony, getting 9 lbs (4 kg). Divide into three unequal parts: say, 2, 3 and 4. Give the small feed before work; the middle one at midday, and the biggest one last thing, when work is finished, and the pony has plenty of time to digest.

Native pony breeds need rather less than the maximum weight-for-height allowance. You could start with 22 lbs (10 kg) for a pure native pony of 14.2 hh. Ponies that have been allowed to get too fat need considerably less; principally, less rich grass. However, to regain their figures, they also want exercise, so they will need some energy food. A small feed of oats is best for them; oats are not in themselves fattening; fat ponies will probably be a bit lazy, so will not become too excitable. Figure-reducing exercise must be regular, and at slow paces: walk and trot. Increase the length of time the pony trots gradually, as it becomes fitter; then, a few short canters. Never try to reduce fat ponies by working them fast straightaway.

Thin ponies need feeding up. They need as much bulk (grass in summer and hay in winter) as they will eat, and several small concentrate feeds each day. Flaked maize, soaked sugar beet, and boiled barley, mixed with bran and cubes will help them. So will cod-liver oil, Solvitax is the veterinary form of this, but don't overdo the amount and give it in one feed only. So also will one of the many vitamin/mineral additives on the market. But a thin pony may also need worming or to have its teeth filed, so consult your vet.

If a pony is off work for any length of time, or is being rested, its concentrate food must be cut right down.

If there's a competition day ahead, when your pony is going to have to be extra energetic, increase its concentrate food the day before; don't give it a *huge* meal the morning of the day itself!

Ponies do not like having their diet changed suddenly. If you want to try a new food mix, or different cubes, introduce the change gradually. Carrots are very good. Feed them sliced as often as you can. All ponies benefit from a salt or mineral lick in their field.

Do not disturb or touch a pony while it is eating – its instinct is to defend itself and its food. It will digest its food better for being left to eat peacefully.

If you want to reward a pony with a titbit after a ride don't give sugar, which is bad for teeth; apples or carrots sliced lengthwise are better.

4 Grooming, foot care and health

Grooming

Grooming makes ponies look nice, but the principal reason for it is to keep their skin and coats healthy. Also, it is when grooming that you can discover if the pony has any cuts, bumps or scratches, and can feel that the coat has no clogged sweat patches, on the back, under the belly, or behind the elbows, where the girth lies. Also, that its mane and tail are not scurfy, and therefore itchy, which will make the pony rub against trees or fences. It is specially important to groom ponies when they are changing their coats; this is called 'casting' the coat, and happens twice a year. In spring or early summer they lose their winter coats and become sleek and fine-coated; in the autumn, they begin to grow their thick protective winter ones again.

Grooming kit

The basic grooming kit you need is: a dandy brush, a body brush, a metal curry comb, a hoof pick, a mane comb and a couple of small sponges or pieces of soft foam rubber. It is useful to have as well a rubber curry comb, a water brush, and a 'stable rubber', although any piece of linen or cotton will do for this.

The dandy brush is for brushing off dirt and mud. If your pony lives out, it is the only one you will need to use on the pony's body in winter. You need to leave some grease in its coat, to keep it warm, and to keep the coat waterproof. The body brush cleans and removes grease; it is the one you should always use, even in winter, on the pony's face, and to brush out its mane and tail. The dandy brush is

A lesson, with the rider sitting quite nicely, although somewhat perched on her 'fork'. The pony is walking out with a good stride, but is 'leaning' on the bit, and is 'on the forehand'.

A Highland Pony stallion in its natural surroundings. This is a very nice pony; the colour is called 'golden dun'.

too hard for its face, and if you use it on mane or tail it tends to break the hairs, and make the mane and tail bristly. The metal curry comb is for cleaning the brushes. You scrape it along the bristles, and then tap the grease or dirt out on to the stable floor, or wall.

The use of the hoof pick is obvious. The mane comb is for the mane and tail, for plaiting and for pulling, which is not done with native ponies as they are protection from the weather. The two small sponges are to wipe the pony's eyes and nostrils when they need it, and to clean under its tail: its 'dock'. Keep the two separate! The rubber curry comb is specially useful when the pony is casting its coat. If you use if firmly, with a sort of massaging movement, you will be surprised at the amount of loose hair that will be freed. The stable rubber is for giving the summer coat a final polish when you want the pony to look specially smart. When you've groomed the pony, fold the cloth into a pad and rub the coat over with it, naturally with the lie of the hair. If the pony comes in wet, or cold, you can use the stable rubber to dry its ears.

Grooming routine

The routine of grooming: start by lifting and picking out the feet. Begin in the corners between the frog and the wall of the hoof and work forwards; and clean out the cleft of the frog. Sweep up the dirt you've picked out. Feet must be picked out every day. With the dandy brush, brush over the body, and brush all dirt and mud off the legs, being careful not to bang them. Feel with your fingers down the legs, and at the back of the pasterns to be sure you've got all the mud off. If this cakes and stays on, it can cause 'mud fever'. This is when the caked mud clogs the pores of the skin, forming small, sometimes large, granulations, which can become very itchy and painful, and if left can make the pony lame.

This pony is jumping well over a 'staircase' type of jump. The rider's seat is too far out of the saddle; she is, however, looking ahead to the next jump and the hands are quite nice; but the standing martingale is too short.

A small child in a 'leading rein' class. The pony is going very nicely, but the small rider's arms are too straight, and the stirrup should be under the ball of the foot, not what is called 'home' (under the instep). Both pony and rider are judged in this class; the rider, for correctness of position, etc, and the pony, for its suitability to be ridden by a small, beginner child.

Here is a pony being brushed with the body brush. Its owner is correctly grooming the left (near) side of the pony with the brush in her left hand, the curry comb (to clean the brush) in her right. When you reach the pony's quarters and your left hand is giving out, it is alright to change to your right! A small detail: she should have slipped the end of the headpiece strap of the headcollar through the keeper, after buckling it.

In spring, summer and early autumn, next take the body brush and really clean the pony. Use some strength as you brush; don't tickle the pony! Start on the left, the 'near' side; use your left hand if you can; even if you find this awkward at first, keep at it, because it strengthens your left arm! You can change hands when you get to the

mane comb

rubber curry comb

metal curry comb

sponge

dandy brush

body brush

water brush

wool
stable bandage
(rolled with tapes
in centre)

hay wisp

hoof pick

stable rubber

tail bandage
(rolled with
tapes in centre)

Grooming kit.

quarters. When you're brushing the pony's quarters and hindlegs, stand *close* to it. It will be harder for it to kick.

Next, undo the headcollar and buckle it round the pony's neck and brush its head and face with the body brush; you will do this even in winter when you are using the dandy on the other parts. Be careful not to bang its face with the back of the brush, or get it into eyes. Now, put the headcollar back on and brush the mane, forelock and the tail. In winter especially, native ponies can manage to get their

37

When picking out a pony's feet, work from the heel to the toe. Be sure to clean out the corners, between the shoe and the heel, around the frog, and the cleft of the frog.

manes and tails into terrific tangles. You will have to work these out with your fingers, and as they have thick manes and tails this may take some time. Be patient, and brush out each bit as you untangle it.

If your pony is living out in winter, you can probably only groom it at weekends. Do try to untangle its mane and tail each weekend, and be very sure you get rid of any caked mud on its legs. If it is a native pony, it will have 'feather', more in winter than in summer: that is, hair on the back of its legs, round its fetlocks and pasterns. Feel with your fingers under the feather and work off any bits of mud you may find there. Pick out its feet. Always, after you have been riding, and specially in winter when the pony may have sweated in its heavier coat, brush its saddle patch and around where the girth lies before turning it out again. In winter use the dandy brush, except for head, mane and tail.

Always use a body brush on the mane and tail. If there are tangles, work them out with your fingers. You can use a mane comb as well, but always finish off the mane by laying it (on the right) with the body brush, or a slightly damped water brush.

Native – Mountain and Moorland – ponies should not be 'trimmed', even for shows. That is: their manes and tails should not be pulled, nor their tails 'banged' (cut straight at the bottom). Nor should their feather be trimmed. The exceptions are Welsh Section B ponies, but

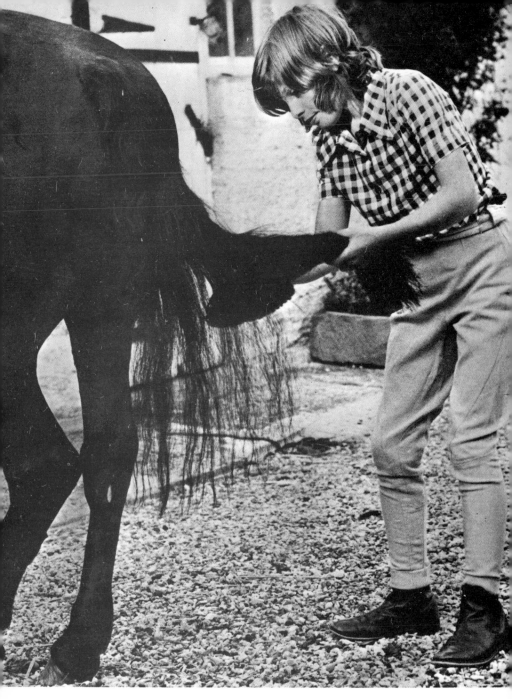

only when shown in Riding Pony classes. The feather is a protection for the legs in winter, so should be left anyway if the pony lives out. There is however nothing against your trying to make your pony's mane and tail as neat as possible, using a water brush. After you have untangled and brushed out the mane, damp the water brush, and use it on the mane to help it to lie flat, on the right hand side of the neck: to 'lay' it. Then damp the top of the tail, and put on a tail bandage until you are ready to go out riding. This will help the tail to lie neatly at the top.

Tails that have got dirty and stained need to be washed; but don't wash them in cold winter weather. For any pony washing (tails, manes, or the removal of dirt stains on the body) always use either pure soap flakes (e.g. Lux), or a special horse or pony shampoo; *not* a detergent. And always rinse out well, with clean water.

If you want your pony to work reasonably hard in the winter and it is living out it can be helpful to have it trace-clipped, when the hair is clipped from the belly, top of the legs and sometimes underneath the neck. This must be done by an expert. It will stop it sweating so much and grooming will be easier. It must then wear a New Zealand rug, except on extremely mild days, until spring (see pages 42, 61 and 62).

Hoof oil makes a pony's feet look smart; it is also good for the hoof; brush it in right up to and round the coronary band, which is where the hoof starts growing, and is like the cuticle of our nails. Put on hoof oil as often as you can.

In summer, when you want to take your pony to a show or a gymkhana, nothing will make its coat glossier, and keep its skin healthier, than really energetic grooming.

Foot care and shoeing
'No foot, no horse', is an old 'horsey' saying, and a very true one. Ponies are just as uncomfortable as people if their shoes don't fit or, if unshod, their feet are not kept properly shaped and trimmed. It is false economy not to let a good farrier attend to your pony's feet regularly, and not to take his advice. For instance, some ponies with good, hard feet, can work perfectly well on soft ground without

Stand to one side of the pony to brush out the tail, and if it is long and tangled, work the tangles out carefully with your fingers, and then brush them. When ponies live out, and have long thick tails, it can take time and patience to untangle them, bit by bit, and then brush them out!

There are several kinds of clip; this is one most often used on ponies in winter, and is a 'trace clip'. It takes the hair away from the places where the pony is most likely to sweat. This is a rather 'high' trace clip. It is often done leaving more coat on the body, only clipping along the belly, between the thighs and forearms, and up the chest and neck and under the throat.

A pony that is trace-clipped in winter will probably need to wear a New Zealand rug if it is living out. This is the traditional waterproofed canvas kind, which will have a woollen lining, and its own surcingle. Notice that the back straps are passed through one another before being fastened back, each on to its own side.

shoes, or with shoes only on their forefeet. Whereas others must always be shod to work in comfort. Most ponies living out in winter and ridden very little are better without their shoes as it gives their feet a chance to grow; some, however, if their hooves are brittle and inclined to crack, need the protection of shoes even then. Only the farrier can tell you these things.

When a pony is in fairly regular work, a set of shoes will last four to six weeks, depending on the kind of ground it is working on. But some ponies are easier on their shoes than others; even after six weeks, their shoes may still be firm and not too worn. All the same, because their *hooves* will have grown in that time, the shoes, although not very worn, will not fit them: the hoof will have grown in places over the shoe. So, to make them comfortable, the farrier will give the pony a 'remove'. That is, he will take off the shoes, reshape the foot, and replace the shoes. Naturally, this costs less. It is therefore wise, when your pony is working, to have the farrier check its feet at least every six weeks.

When you pick out your pony's feet, you should check that its shoes are firm, that none has become twisted or pulled too much to one side. The nails which hold the shoes in place, and which are turned over and down on the outside of the hoof, are called the 'clenches'. When those clenches are no longer absolutely flat against the hoof, they are said to have 'risen'. When this happens it is a sign that the shoes are becoming less firmly fixed, and they need doing, however recently they were done.

The frog is an important part of the pony's foot; it is resilient: a sort of shock absorber. One reason why you pick out your pony's feet is to be sure the frog is clean, no dirt or dung left in the cleft. Dung is very heating. If it is left in the foot and in the cleft of the frog, it will soften the sole of the foot, and cause a sort of rot of the frog, called 'thrush'. It is mostly stabled ponies kept in dirty boxes and always standing in dung that get thrush. It is a preventable complaint; a well cared-for pony should never get it. So, don't neglect your foot-cleaning routine!

Every time you pick out your pony's feet, insist that it stands quietly. This will be a help to your farrier; he finds nothing more time-wasting or annoying than a pony which won't stand still to be shod. Get it thoroughly used to 'foot care', and to standing on three legs without fussing. Hold the pony for him yourself, although when the pony gets to know him, it will probably stand quietly on its own, tied

Here you can see distinctly the 'clenches', the nails which hold the shoe in place. When these are no longer lying flat against the hoof, they are said to be 'risen', and this is a sign the shoes are becoming loose and worn, and the pony needs the attention of the farrier. This is a forefoot; these shoes are put on with a 'clip' centre front. Hind shoes often have a clip on either side instead of in the centre.

to a ring and nibbling at a hay net. If the pony has any awkwardness of action, tell the farrier and let him see it walk and trot. He may be able to improve it with special shoes. Watch your farrier at work; ask him questions. He is a highly skilled craftsman from whom you can learn a lot.

General health

Learn to recognize the signs of a pony in good health both in appearance and behaviour, and train yourself to spot when it is 'off-colour'. A healthy pony should always be alert, bright eyed, ears pricking to and fro. Its coat, whether winter or summer, should lie flat, and the skin be soft and supple. When standing, while the pony

44

may and often will rest a hindleg, it never rests a foreleg unless there is something wrong with the leg or the foot. The membranes – that is, the linings – of its eyes and nostrils should be a clear salmon pink.

The normal temperature is 100°F (37.7°C); its pulse rate about 40 beats to the minute; its breathing, about 15 breaths to the minute. Both these rates increase with exercise, fright, or excitement. The temperature is taken by lifting its tail and slipping the thermometer into the rectum. Grease the end of the thermometer first. If you are ever uncertain of whether or not your pony needs the vet, take its temperature; if it is over 101°F (38.3°C), send for him. The pulse is not easy for an amateur to find; if you are interested, ask your vet to show you where to look for it next time he calls.

A pony that is not in good health will stand with drooping head, dull eyes and listless ears. Its coat may be 'staring': that is, the hairs instead of lying flat, will stand away from the body. It will probably have drawn its quarters under it, appearing rather hunched. Sadly, many ponies that are turned out in winter, and neglected, get into this condition; party because they have not enough to eat, partly because they are probably infested with worms (see page 49).

The medicine chest
You don't need to keep an elaborate medicine chest for your pony.

The basic necessities are: A thermometer. A container of antiseptic dusting powder. A jar or tube of healing ointment: a good proprietary one is called 'Protocon'. A small cake of medicated soap. A bottle of mild disinfectant. A three foot long (1 metre) crepe bandage, the same as for humans. A few pieces of clean linen or cotton, for pads or for putting on poultices. A tin of kaolin poultice. A pair of sharp, blunt ended scissors, (in case you have to cut the hairs away from the edges of a cut, to stop the hair turning into the cut as it heals). Anything else you may need at any time the vet will provide. If you ask him, he will also leave you the necessary worm doses for your pony, and tell you when to give them. Your salt-and-water solution you can make as you need it.

Minor ailments
If anything seems to be really wrong with your pony, you must call in your veterinary surgeon. Keep his telephone number written up in your tack room, or by the telephone, so you can ring him quickly in an emergency. But there are some minor ailments, or minor mishaps,

45

with which you should know how to cope, even if only till the vet can get to you.

Cuts and scratches

These should be cleaned with a few drops of a mild disinfectant in tepid water, then dusted with an antiseptic powder, and left open to the air. If a cut is more than skin deep, the sides sprung rather far apart, you should call the vet as it may need stitching. In the meantime, bathe with mild disinfectant in cold water, to help stop the bleeding. If it is on a leg (most cuts are) make a thick pad of clean linen and bandage it in place till the vet comes.

Puncture wounds

These are more difficult. They are caused by something sharp: a nail or a thorn, maybe – going into the flesh, often leaving no mark, but there will be a hot swelling caused by trapped poison, or dirt. Clean this by putting on a hot kaolin poultice. Put the hot kaolin on to a pad of clean white cloth; wrap paper or polythene round it to keep the heat in, and bandage. Repeat the poulticing until the pad comes off clean with no pus on it. Consult your vet about any puncture wound.

Girth galls

If you keep your girths clean and your pony's coat free from clogged sweat, the pony should never develop girth galls. However, if it is rather fat and out of condition at the start of the summer holidays, you may find, when you brush it after riding, a softish lump just behind its elbows. This is the beginning of a girth gall which will get bigger if you do nothing about it, and which the continued friction of the girth will turn into an open sore. Stop riding the pony for a few days and bathe the lump with a solution of salt and water. Put two tablespoons of salt into a lemonade bottle, fill with water and shake, and sponge it on to the lump. In a week, possibly less, the lump will have gone down, and the salt and water will have hardened the skin so that the lump should not re-form.

Be sure, when you ride again, that the skin is flat under the girth. When you have done up the girths, take each foreleg in turn and pull it forward; this straightens out any skin wrinkles there may have been under the girth. It is a good thing to do this always, but specially when ponies are rather fat, or may have some thick winter coat left. It is also a good thing, if your pony has been out of work for some time, to

46

sponge the girth area and the back where the saddle lies, with salt and water to help prevent the rather soft skin being rubbed into galls.

Saddle galls

Saddle galls are caused by badly fitting, or worn, saddles; also by sloppy riders who don't sit still but keep on shifting their weight about. If you find a lump on the pony's back which causes the pony to 'dip' its back when you press on it, stop riding, and check your saddle. Take it to a good saddler. It may need re-stuffing; the tree may be broken, or, if it is a cheap foreign saddle, it may have been made on a mis-shapen tree. Bathe the lump with salt and water. Do not ride again until it has subsided, and until you are sure your saddle fits properly. And – check your own riding position! Put a thick, soft numnah under the saddle when you first ride again, and sit still, and straight, when you're on top.

Lameness

If your pony suddenly goes lame on a ride, get off, and lift the foot on which it is lame to see if it has picked up a stone. This is a common cause of sudden lameness and very easily cured, by removing the stone. If there is no stone, run up your stirrups, and walk the pony home. If you ride the pony you may make the sprain, or whatever has caused the lameness, so much worse that the pony will have to be laid off for quite a long time.

When you get home, put the pony into a box or stable, if possible, with some bedding. You can't be expected to know a lot about the tendons and ligaments of a pony's legs, so just put a cold water bandage on to the leg, and ask the vet to come. A slight sprain or strain usually comes right fairly quickly with liniment, or a kaolin poultice, put on under a support bandage, and with rest. Rest doesn't necessarily mean keeping the pony in; it means *not riding it*. Always take your vet's advice. If he says you should rest the pony for two, three, or more, weeks, don't, just because it seems all right to you, start riding again before the time is up.

Colic

Colic is acute indigestion. It is more serious for ponies than it is for us, because they cannot relieve themselves by being sick! A pony that has colic will be very restless and in obvious pain. It will lie down, roll; get up, look round at its stomach, lie down again, probably sweat. Its stomach may look rather swollen and distended, and although it may lift its tail hopefully, it will be unable to pass dung. If you put your ear to its sides, you will hear no rumblings going on: its insides have become so congested that they are no longer working. It will also, naturally, be off its food. If you ever suspect that your pony may have colic, do please send for the vet, and in the meantime, halter the pony and keep it walking about until he comes, and have its box ready for it, as he may tell you to keep it in after treatment.

Laminitis

Laminitis is fever of the feet, and very painful. It can be prevented by making sure that ponies, especially small native ones, do not eat too much rich grass in spring and summer, or eat too much at any time when not in regular exercise. A pony that has laminitis needn't look specially fat, but it will stand with its forelegs stretched out in front of it, all the weight on its heels, because it is painful to put the whole foot on the ground. The vet will help you to treat it, but he will certainly tell you to keep the pony in, to give it a very sparse diet, to take it short walks daily and probably, if you have a stream or river nearby, to stand it in the water for a time each day. Laminitis is curable, but ponies that have once had it are likely to get it again. You have to be extra careful never to let them over-eat.

Colds and coughs

Ponies get colds in the head just as we do, but fortunately, not nearly so often. The symptoms are the same: runny noses, and sometimes a cough. Colds are infectious, so if your pony lives out with others and has a runny nose, you really should take it out of that field if you can, keeping it in its box and taking it out for walks, or for slow daily exercise. Wipe the nostrils clean with bits of cotton wool then throw them away. If it has a cough, as well, you should call the vet, who will probably give you a 'cough electuary'. This usually has a treacle base, so ponies tend to like it; it is given from a spatula, like a flat wooden spoon, or off an ordinary kitchen wooden spoon. A pony with a cough should not be worked at all until it stops coughing.

There are however different kinds of cough. If your pony, either in the stable or when it first comes out, gives a little short cough and then blows its nose, it is probably simply getting rid of a tickle in its throat or a bit of hay which got stuck there. Constant coughing requires the vet's attention.

48

Worms

Worms are the most common cause of ponies losing condition, even well-fed ones. The most dangerous kind are redworms, so small you cannot see them in the droppings, and so called because they suck blood. They can eat through the lining of the stomach and of the intestines, and can cause death. Your pony should be wormed at least four times a year. Consult your vet.

Lice

Other unpleasant parasites which can appear even on well cared-for ponies living out, especially native ones with thick manes and tails, are lice. If your pony seems specially itchy, always rubbing its mane and tail, look carefully into the roots of the hair of the mane, forelock and tail. If you see anything that looks like scurf but is actually moving, get a good louse powder and dust it thickly into the mane and tail, and along the spine. Do this for several days running; then shampoo, then dust again, and you should have finished the creatures off.

Itchiness

A more ordinary cause of itchiness is overheated blood in spring or summer, from rich grass. Brush and shampoo mane and tail, and give the pony about two tablespoons of Epsom Salts in its daily concentrate feed, which should be made fairly wet. Rich food which overheats the blood can also make some ponies come out into little pimples over their bodies: a sort of heat rash. Epsom Salts given in rather wet feeds will help this too. Incidentally, when you ask the chemist for Epsom Salts, tell him you want it for your pony, partly because he will think it peculiar if you ask for a pound without explaining why you want so much; partly because he will then sell you the special kind made up for animals, which comes in pounds, not ounces, and is also cheaper!

49

5 Tack, pony clothing and riding clothes

Tack, short for 'tackle', is the word used to describe all the equipment worn by riding horses and ponies. That worn by driving horses is called harness. Boots, bandages and rugs are called horse clothing.

To ride a pony, the basic tack you need is a bridle, a saddle, girths, and stirrup leathers and irons.

The saddle

The most important is the saddle, because it must fit both you and the pony. Saddles are made with a fairly wide channel or gullet, between the padding on either side. This is to keep the saddle from pressing on the pony's spine. Therefore, the first thing to make sure of is that when the saddle is on the pony's back, this channel is free. You should be able to see daylight through it, from back to front. Then, the front of the saddle, called the pommel, should not press down on the pony's withers. You should be able to put all four fingers between the pommel and the pony.

Ponies are of very different shapes, and widths. So saddles are also made in different widths of trees. The tree is the wooden 'skeleton' around which the saddle is constructed. There are three widths: narrow, medium and wide. Most native ponies take a medium width; some of the larger breeds, the wide one; a finely-bred show pony may take the narrow. The width of the tree matters a lot. If it is too narrow, the saddle will sit up on the pony's back, and when you sit on it, will pinch its sides. Too wide a tree will sit down, and you won't be able to get your fingers between the pommel and the pony. The only way to be sure a saddle fits a particular pony is to put it on, and then

Bending poles; one of the most popular gymkhana games. For these you don't need a jacket; shirt and tie, or a sweater, are more sensible, and are always worn.

get up on it. It may look all right until you mount; your weight may alter the way it fits. Ask an expert to advise you.

To be comfortable for you, when you sit in the saddle, you should feel you can sit easily upright, with no sensation of being tilted either backwards or forwards. Saddles today are better designed than they used to be. Their deep seats, narrow waists and fairly high cantles help you to sit in the correct, and most comfortable, position. The seat of the saddle must also be big enough to accommodate yours! You should be able to put the flat of your hand behind you on the cantle. Saddles are measured lengthwise from front to back, the size being the length from the pommel to the cantle. Small children need a small, 14 or 15 inch (35 or 37 cm) saddle; a 16 inch (40 cm) is usually big enough for older children or young teenagers; but if you have a large behind and perhaps rather fat thighs, you will need a 17 inch (42 cm) one. It is more uncomfortable to ride on too small a saddle than on one a little too big.

In the old days, most saddles were made with padded full panels. Today, although some have 'half panels', the best ones have what is called the 'continental panel', which is simply two thicknesses of leather, and which lets you feel much closer to the pony.

There are different saddles designed for special purposes. Dressage saddles have very deep seats and long straight panels. Jumping saddles have the panels very forward cut, and knee and thigh rolls. Showing saddles have straight panels like dressage ones but not so deep-seated. For all-round use there is the 'general purpose' saddle. Few people can afford more than one saddle, so the 'general purpose' is the one to choose. It is exactly what it says. It has a deep seat, a long, slightly forward-cut panel, knee and thigh rolls but not nearly so pronounced as on the jumping saddle. You can 'ride long', that is, with long stirrups, on it for schooling or for your dressage test; you can pull up your stirrups for jumping or riding across country, and unless your *only* interest is showing, it is a perfectly good show saddle. The Pony Club has designed a saddle which is made by different saddlers to the same pattern. These are more or less general purpose ones, and not too wildly expensive. Saddles are made on spring trees or rigid trees. Children's saddles usually have rigid trees.

Pony Club camp is an ideal opportunity for having fun.

It is not necessary to buy the most expensive saddle on the market, even if you can afford it. On the other hand, it is not wise to buy a very cheap one, because it is probably of unknown origin and make; it will not last, and no reputable saddler will, or can, repair it when it starts to fall to pieces. A good second-hand saddle is a very good buy, because it is already soft and 'ridden in'. Most saddlers have second-hand saddles from time to time, because when people buy new horses or ponies, they often need new saddles to fit them, and turn their old ones in for resale. If you do buy a new saddle, after about a year you should take it back to the saddler for him to check the padding; your weight will have flattened it down.

Girths
The principle kinds of girth are: nylon, webbing, leather, lampwick and Cottage Craft. Nylon is easy to wash and quick to dry, but has no give,

Types of girth, from left: webbing, used in pairs for safety; nylon; Balding; lampwick; Fitzwilliam; tubular linen, for showing; and three-fold leather.

This is a sensible way to carry your tack: the bridle over your shoulder, with the reins looped up over the headpiece so that they don't trail on the ground; and the saddle over your arm, the stirrups 'run up'. This rider is carrying her tack to the pony to put it on. If you are taking it off, you do not need to undo both sides of the girth; you undo the left (near) side, and as you take the saddle off, you bring the girth over the top of the saddle from the right (off) side.

and if pulled up tight does not always lie flat. Webbing girths must be used in pairs and kept clean of sweat and hairs; they can be dangerous, as with wear they can split without warning. Leather girths are excellent, but must be well cared-for. Folded leather ones are put on with the fold to the front, and should have a piece of oiled cloth laid inside them. Those with shaped strips of leather coming behind the elbows are called Balding girths; those that are stitched and shaped, Atherstone. The easiest to keep clean, as they can be washed, are lampwick and Cottage Craft. Both are of soft material, dry quickly, and are sweat absorbent.

Stirrups
Stirrup leathers should always be of good quality leather. These are made in different lengths. Be sensible and get the length that has some relation to that of your own legs! You don't want to have a lot of spare leather hanging down; nor do you want to run out of holes when you grow and your legs get longer.

Stirrup irons should be fairly heavy, made of stainless steel or solid nickel and be about an inch (2.5 cm) wider than your booted foot. Too narrow, you wouldn't be able to get your foot out if you happened to fall; too wide, your foot could slip right through the iron. Rubber treads fitted to the stirrups help your feet to stay in place and keep them warmer in winter.

The bridle
Ponies should not need anything other than a bridle with a plain cavesson noseband, and some form of snaffle bit. Bridles are made in sizes: pony, cob, and full size; extra small ones for Shetlands and some Welsh Mountains. Big ponies, Fells, Dales and Highlands usually need cob size. Be sure the throatlash is long enough. Don't get fancy reins. Unless, or until, you become a very good rider and compete in cross-country events and need reins that give you a better hold, particularly in the wet, the plain leather ones that are sold with the bridle are all you want.

Types of bit
There are two basic kinds of bit: the snaffle, and the curb. The snaffle works on the principle of 'direct action': from the rider's hand to the lips and the bars of the horse's mouth. The curb works on what is called 'leverage'. The bit has long 'cheeks', to which the reins are attached, and at the other end, the cheekpieces of the bridle are fitted on to small rings. When there is pressure on the reins, the rein cheek comes back; the bridle one, forward: this puts pressure on the horse's poll – the top of his head – causing him to lower it.

Everyone should start riding with a snaffle. There are different designs of snaffle, and two distinct kinds: snaffles without joints in

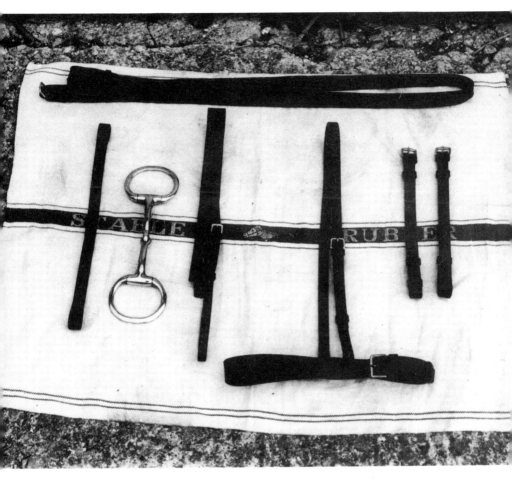

The parts of a snaffle bridle. At the top, the reins; from left: browband; bit, an eggbutt snaffle; headpiece with the throatlash buckled up; noseband; and cheekpieces.

the middle, called 'mullen-mouth'; and snaffles with joints, called simply 'jointed snaffles'.

A 'LOOSE RING' jointed snaffle has the ring going through a hole each end of the mouthpiece; therefore the ring can slip round. In an EGGBUTT snaffle, the ring cannot slip round as it is joined to the mouthpiece by a smooth piece of metal. Snaffles are also made of RUBBER and VULCANITE; these are good for young ponies. Snaffles can also have cheekpieces; these are called FULMER snaffles. 'GERMAN' snaffles have thicker mouthpieces, and come in all three designs: loose ring, eggbutt, and Fulmer.

STRAIGHT BAR, or 'MULLEN-MOUTH' snaffles are the mildest bits of all, because even if the rider's hand is unsteady, the bit will stay resting on the bars of the mouth. With jointed snaffles, unsteady or rough hands jerking on the bit can make the joint jump upwards, like a nutcracker, and bang against the roof of the horse's mouth.

The eggbutt snaffle is the one in most general use, and is probably the best for your original buy. But do remember that ponies have mouths of very different WIDTHS! The bit you buy should fit the width of your pony's mouth, from corner to corner. If it is too wide, it will slip from side to side, even if it is an eggbutt, and will worry the pony, because you won't be able to keep an even feel on both reins. If it is too narrow, it will pinch the corners of the pony's mouth, and may even rub the corners raw. The average width for ponies between 13 hh and 14.2 hh is 5 inches (12.5 cm); smaller ones will need less width, and heavier ones, like Fells, Dales or Highlands, probably need 5½ inches (14 cm).

The PELHAM can be a useful bit for ponies. It has a single mouthpiece, but is made to be used with two reins: snaffle and curb. The usually unjointed mouthpiece has cheeks, to which the curb rein is attached, and rings level with the mouthpiece, which take the snaffle reins. It is worn with a curb chain. There is really no point in using a Pelham unless you know how to ride with two reins, without being muddled as to which is which. If you are being taught to ride with two reins it is a good idea to practise by putting two reins on to an ordinary snaffle, and get used to having so much leather in your hands. When adjusting a curb chain it should be twisted until the links of the chain, when you hook it on, are lying quite flat. There are different kinds of curb chain, some mild, some more severe.

Another bit which can be useful is the KIMBLEWICK, which is a very mild form of curb, worn with a curb chain but used with one rein. This has an unjointed mouthpiece, with a 'port', – a rounded hump – in the centre.

DOUBLE BRIDLES are only for very competent riders, and well-schooled ponies. They have two bits: a snaffle, which is called the 'bridoon', (sometimes called bradoon) and a curb, which is called the 'bit'. Many ponies have rather small mouths and find a double bridle rather a lot of ironmongery to cope with. Although at big shows it is customary to show ponies in a double bridle, small-mouthed ones will probably go better in a Pelham, which is perfectly acceptable. The use of a Pelham bit is now perfectly acceptable in some Pony Club dressage tests. Adults, however, still have to use snaffles in both Preliminary and Novice dressage tests.

The only other absolutely necessary tack you will need for your own pony is a headcollar, and a rope that has a clip end. Leather headcollars are very expensive now; there are lots of gaily coloured nylon ones that are strong and efficient, and easy to keep clean, as they can be washed.

Martingales, drop, flash and Grakle nosebands, are all 'extras', which there's no need to buy until the day comes when you think you may need one of them. The chances are, you never will. And if you wonder why I haven't mentioned numnahs, it is because your saddle should fit your pony. If it does, there is no need to stick a numnah under it. If you do fancy a numnah, probably because all your friends have one, don't get too thick a one, and *do* keep it clean!

Tack is very expensive, but if it is well looked after, it will last a very long time. I had a saddle which lasted me for 35 years, with attention when necessary from the saddler, and was still in good enough condition for me to part-exchange it for a more modern one.

Cleaning tack
Never forget to clean your tack every time you use it; never put it away wet, after a ride in the rain. Try to be methodical about this. Never use HOT water; only just tepid, and don't get the leather too wet when cleaning it; use a damp, squeezed-out, not a sopping wet, sponge. The same when putting on saddle soap; you don't want a foaming lather; use as little moisture as possible and work the soap well in. It shouldn't leave soapy bits stuck in the buckle holes. Clean tack should feel cool, supple, and non-sticky. Important places to keep clean are where the leather comes into contact with metal: where the cheekpieces fit on to the bit, and where the stirrup lies in the irons.

Check all the stitching on the bridle, and at the top of the stirrup leathers every time you clean your tack. If any seems to be giving way, get it repaired at once. A local shoemaker will often repair stitching for you if the saddler can't do it immediately.

A new saddle needs a lot of softening. You can use neatsfoot oil on the underside of the panels and on the girth tabs; or use a good

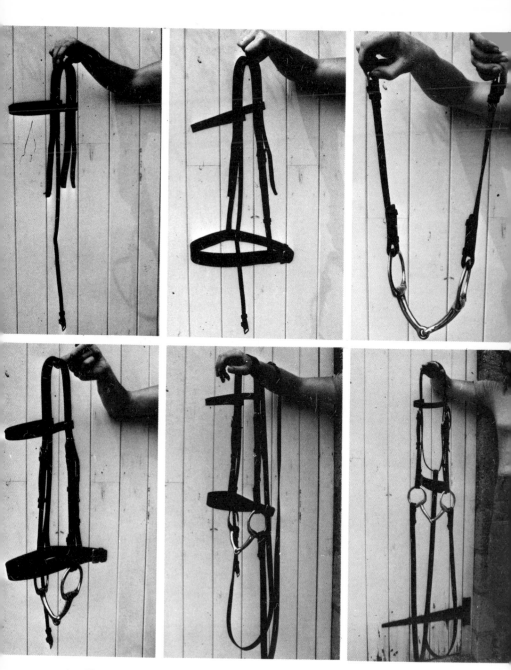

preparation called Kocholine, which you should work in with your fingers. Don't use this on the seat, or the outside of the panels, though, as it will stain your clothes. Everyone likes to see the outside of their saddle clean and glowing; but it is the underside of the leather that is the most absorbent because it is 'undressed'.

Provided that at least twice a week you take your bridle apart, and 'strip' your saddle (that is, take off the leathers and irons and clean them separately) there is no need to do this after every ride, unless everything has got wet or particularly dirty. Wipe it over with a damp sponge or cloth, then, with another sponge, work in a little soap or dressing.

When not in use tack should be 'put up' tidily. The bridle should go on a special rack or a block of wood shaped to fit under the headpiece, or a saddle soap tin nailed up, preferably high enough so the reins can hang down straight. Otherwise they should be looped up on the throatlash. The saddle should go on a rack or saddlehorse but failing that can be propped up resting on the pommel. It should never rest on the cantle or lie flat as this could damage it. Stirrup irons should be run up and the girth left unbuckled lying across the saddle.

If you have a native, Mountain and Moorland pony, or one that grows a thick coat in winter, the only *horse clothing* which you should need is a set of bandages, and a tail bandage. The bandages may be useful should the pony go lame, and need their support while resting, or should you want to take it anywhere in a trailer. The tail bandage will help to make its tail lie neat and flat if you put it on after grooming on days when you want it to look specially smart. The pony will also need to wear it, should it travel.

Ponies living out that do not grow very thick coats in winter or that are trace-clipped will need New Zealand rugs. These are made of

How to put your bridle together. First, pass the short straps of the headpiece through the loops of the browband, so that the long part of the throatlash is on the right, and will therefore buckle on the left.

Then, pass the long strap of the noseband from right to left through the underside of the browband loops, so that this also will buckle to the left.

Then, attach the bit to the cheekpieces. If your bridle has stud fastenings, these go to the inside. If it has buckles at the bit end, these go to the outside.

Now, buckle the cheekpieces on to the headpiece.

Finally, attach the reins to the bit, behind the cheekpieces. Again: if stud fastenings, these to the inside; if buckles, to the outside.

To put the bridle away tidily, loop the throatlash round the reins and buckle it; take the noseband round the outside of the cheekpieces and buckle it.

61

waterproof canvas with blanket linings, or of various man-made materials. Some have to be worn with surcingles. However, the best are so made that they can be worn without. Rugs are made in different sizes, and the measurement is taken from the front of the chest in a straight line to the quarters. It is important that they FIT. New Zealand rugs should be removed, checked and replaced daily. Sheepskin padding at the withers will prevent rubbing.

Riding clothes

When you start riding it is not necessary to buy a lot of expensive clothes. Although you should always look clean and tidy when riding, remember that clothes do not make the rider!

The two essentials, whatever kind of riding you do, are a hard hat and sensible footwear; either jodhpur boots or lace-up shoes with sole and heel: NOT platform soles or Wellingtons (although green 'Hunter' ones are permissable), and never gym shoes or 'trainers'. Ride in cords or a pair of comfortable trousers. Wear jeans only at home: never wear trousers that are too tight or which rub your legs. If you have jodhpurs, you may feel you want long rubber boots. In fact, the correct wear with jodhpurs is jodhpur boots; long boots are really for breeches. Rubber boots have one advantage, which is that you can mess around in the stable in them, and just wash them off, whereas working in the stable or tidying a muck heap in leather boots or shoes is not good for the leather. But, unlike leather boots, which are now wildly expensive, rubber ones are cold in winter and hot in summer. Small children should definitely *not* wear rubber boots. Jodhpur boots with straps are probably better than those with elastic, which will go soft in time and cannot be replaced.

If you're riding mostly at home, you can wear any sort of jacket or anorak you fancy and that will keep you warm and dry. For any other riding, except showing or competitive events, quilted jackets or waistcoats are permissible; their advantage being that you can wear them when you are not riding. A riding mac is worth saving up for, as it is tough and has straps to go round your legs.

If you are going to start riding you must have a hat that fits you. Apart from that, if you are wearing either a clean shirt or a polo neck sweater, tough trousers or jodphurs with jodhpur boots or sensible shoes, and if cold, a quilted jacket or waistcoat, you will not be sent home from a riding school in disgrace because you do not have a 'hacking jacket' or rubber boots. String gloves are a good

You don't have to be very grown up, or have a very grand pony, to go hunting or drag-hunting. This rider is on a sensible pony, which she is controlling with a simple snaffle bridle. She is wearing quite ordinary clothes: jodhpurs, jodhpur boots, a neat jacket, and a riding hat, nothing elaborate or expensive.

idea for warmth and to stop the reins chafing in wet weather – in cream, fawn or yellow.

In other words, you can add to your riding clothing as you or your parents can afford, and according to the kind of riding you are doing. Casual clothes should be in quiet colours, not garishly bright, though.

For showing, the correct wear for anyone under 16 is: a hat, black,

Here is a Welsh Pony who has won a rosette in a Mountain and Moorland Ridden Class, ridden in a Pelham. The pony is beautifully groomed, its tail neatly banged. The rider is well turned-out in a neat jacket; jodhpurs and jodhpur boots, her hair in a net and clean gloves.

brown or dark blue. A shirt and tie; jodhpurs and jodhpur boots, a hacking jacket, and *gloves*. The same for the dressage and the show jumping section of Pony Club competitions, except that you can leave the gloves off if you want to, and that you must wear an approved hat with a secured chinstrap. For cross-country riding you must wear a crash helmet with chinstrap. Most people ride cross-country in striped sweat shirts of various colours. Here, you can wear rubber boots if you want to, to protect your legs.

A tip; if you're going to a show and don't want to bother changing into clean jodhpurs when you get there, put a pair of loose jeans on over them for travelling.

Whatever kind of footwear you ride in, be sure it is comfortable, and not too tight. In winter, riding can be very cold on the feet, especially if your boots or shoes are tight. If they are a half size bigger than you normally wear, you will be able both to put thick woolly socks on, and to wiggle your toes about. The same goes for gloves. Give your fingers room to move, and your hands will stay warmer. It is not good form to wear long socks turned down over the tops of the boots!

A final word; please, at all times, keep your hair tidy! Tie it back or wear a hairnet if it is long.

6 Riding and owning a pony

Not everyone who is fond of ponies can own one, but naturally, if you like ponies, you want to ride. Like any sport riding has certain rules which you must learn if you are going to enjoy it. Some people learn quickly because they have a natural gift. But there is a right and a wrong way to ride, and unless you start the right way, you will never be able to make the pony understand what you want it to do, and neither of you will enjoy yourselves. Riding, although it has to be learnt, is unlike any other sport, in that it is a partnership; between yourself and the pony, who should like being ridden as much as you like riding it.

You should therefore persuade your parents to let you have some riding lessons, or save up your pocket money or wages. Generally, lessons do not cost more than a lesson in any other sport. And remember, apart from a hat, you do not need expensive clothes. Some riding schools will lend or hire hats, but it is better to have your own. If you're going to spend money on riding lessons, you must be sure you are really going to be *taught*. So you should go to a school that is 'approved' (see pages 94 and 99). It will have reliable, sensible ponies, which will give you confidence.

Don't think, however, that on your first lesson, you will be cantering about or jumping! You have to learn how to mount, and dismount; how to sit correctly in the saddle and how to hold your reins, and you will have to learn 'the aids': the methods by which you communicate your wishes to the pony. If you are keen, you will listen to, and try to do, everything you are told, when it should not take you long before you are able to sit comfortably on the pony, and control it at walk, trot, and canter.

When you have reached this stage, you are ready to accept the offer of a ride on a friend's pony. Or if you see a pony doing nothing in a field, you could find out who owns it, approach them, and ask if you

Here are some of the implements which are used round a stable, and which, if you go to help at a riding school, you should know about. On the left is a long handled fork, for mucking out and laying beds. In some places, you might use a 'pitchfork', which is a long handled fork with two prongs, when you would also use a short handled fork for picking up soiled straw. The broom is for sweeping the floor of the boxes after mucking out, and sweeping the yard: a chore which is very necessary if the yard is to look neat and tidy. The shovel is for picking up the muck; the wheelbarrow, for collecting the muck, and taking it to the manure heap, useful too for carrying sacks of footstuffs. It is also useful to have a 'skip': a wire or plastic basket into which droppings can be put when tidying a box and for catching the dirt when you are picking out a pony's feet.

may be allowed to ride it. But never overestimate your own ability. Do not take risks. Not all ponies will be as well-mannered as the riding school ones. If a pony doesn't immediately do what you want, don't blame the pony. Remember all the things you were taught, try to do them correctly, and try, at walk, to get the pony relaxed and paying attention to you. Ponies can seem to be stubborn or naughty, when what is wrong with them is that they have been ridden by rough, or bad, riders. If you are quiet and tactful they will be so surprised and pleased that most will end by going nicely for you.

Never think that you have come to the end of learning to ride. The best riders in the world go on instructional and refresher courses. Take every chance you can of having lessons.

The one thing you should never do is ride a pony without the owner's consent. If you see ponies in a field, don't be tempted to go in, and jump on one bareback. That you may be bucked off doesn't matter. What does matter is the harm, even the fright, you may give the pony which for all you know, may be only a youngster, apart from the fact that you could get into trouble for trespassing.

It is worth asking at your riding school if you may come and help round the yard. But remember: helping means *working*, not leaning over your favourite pony's box, feeding it endless polo mints! The yard has to be swept, boxes mucked out, beds laid, the muck heap tidied, haynets filled, and tack cleaned; dull jobs, you may think at first, but they all have to be done. Later you may be shown how to do more interesting ones; how to catch and bring back ponies from the field; how to groom, put tack on properly, and take it off, clean and put it away at the end of a ride. If you become a reliable and trustworthy helper, always turning up when you say and finishing a job before leaving, you may now and then be rewarded with a free lesson or ride. You will learn a lot; keep a notebook and write down things. If people see that you're interested they won't mind if you ask them questions when they are not busy.

A good way to enjoy ponies is to go for a trekking or a riding holiday. Many are specially for young people, and children. They seldom cost any more than other holidays. Practically all are 'package holidays'; the weekly charge covering absolutely everything. Trekking can be fun, but is always done at slow paces, because people who have never sat on a pony before go trekking. There may be some gentle trotting, but seldom any cantering. At most centres, everyone is allocated a pony to ride, and look after, for their stay. Many riding holiday establishments cater for complete beginners who are given progressive lessons, while experienced riders do more advanced riding. There are also riding schools which offer holiday courses, with instruction and riding geared to individual riders' capabilities. The horsey magazines advertise a wide variety of these.

Provided you have a hard hat and sensible shoes, you can go trekking in tough trousers, a sweater and an anorak. For a riding holiday you should have jodhpurs. You need enough changes of clothes; holiday weather can be wet.

It is most important to choose an establishment which is approved: by the Ponies of Britain, the British Horse Society, the Association of British Riding Schools, or by the Sports Council, or Trekking Association, of the particular country. They will send lists of approved establishments. The Irish Tourist Board can tell you about riding and trekking in Ireland (see Societies and useful addresses).

The Horse Rangers Associaton

This is an organization specially for children who do not have their own ponies. It aims to train members not only in riding, but in all branches of horse care and stable management. The headquarters are in Surrey and there are eight branches. Boys and girls from 6 upwards can belong. Young ones are called Junior Rangers. The older and more proficient Rangers are expected to help whenever they can with Riding for the Disabled (see page 95 and Societies and useful addresses). The member's subscription is entirely dependent on what you can afford to pay; however much or little that may be, you get the same amount of riding and training. So if you are enthusiastic and have no pony, write to the headquarters for information (see Societies and useful addresses). As the Association organizes progressive riding and horsemastership tests, trained by them you could go on to become a good enough rider and horsemaster to work professionally with horses if you wanted to.

The Pony Club

The Pony Club, now over 50 years old and worldwide, is a wonderful organization. It gives children the opportunity of becoming good riders without having to pay a lot for lessons. If you're lucky enough to have a pony, you should join; or your riding school may hire you one for Pony Club events. You will learn a lot very enjoyably, especially at the annual Pony Club camps. But don't get discontented with your pony because others are better looking, or be too keen to win a lot of competitions. In all branches, there will be some specially talented riders who will be in the teams for the Inter Branch Cross Country, Show Jumping and Dressage. You may be one of them. If you

69

If you have a pony of your own or can hire one regularly, you should join your nearest branch of the Pony Club. As well as learning a lot about riding, and pony care, you will have fun riding with others, and make new friends. Here is a group at a Pony Club rally.

are not, don't envy them; get on with learning all you can about riding and pony care, and make the best of the pony you have. If it's small and active, and you are under 15, you may be chosen to take part in the Prince Philip Cup Games. Tough, hardy, agile and clever small ponies are much better at gymkhana games than larger, highly bred, and more expensive ones! Write to the Headquarters to find your nearest branch (see Societies and useful addresses).

A pony of your own

To own a pony is a responsibility. A pony isn't a toy which you can forget about when you don't want to play with it; nor is it like a dog, which if you forget to feed it will remind you by barking. Your pony will be entirely dependent on you for its food, care, comfort and general well-being. Keeping it is going to cost not only money, but time.

Not all of us can keep ponies at our homes. They cannot be kept in back gardens or woodsheds or in partitioned-off bits of the garage. If you live in the country you may be able to rent a field, or find a friendly farmer who will let the pony graze with his sheep or cattle. If you cannot find grazing you will have to find a stables where the pony can be kept at livery. This needn't be expensive. If the school has some land, the pony can be kept at 'grass livery'; that is, 'living out'; the school providing hay in winter, or when necessary, the owner providing the concentrate feeds and the owner also catching the pony, grooming it and tacking it up before riding.

If the stable has no land, there is 'half livery'. That is, the school can use the pony when the owner doesn't want to ride it. There are snags to this. The school may when busy use the pony rather too much, or put too many novice riders on it, so that it gets bored and forgets the schooling the owner is trying to give it! It is sensible, at 'half livery', to stipulate the numbers of hours a week the pony can be used by the school. Whatever livery charge is agreed, the owner is always expected to pay for the pony's shoeing, and for any vet's bills that may arise.

The ideal is for two friends to keep their ponies together; sharing the cost of the hay and the grazing and each buying their own concentrate feeds. Not only is it fun to be able to ride out together, but if one of you gets ill, or has to go away, the other can look after both ponies.

Handling, looking after and generally being with your pony should give you just as much pleasure as riding it. Therefore, it is important that it should have a kindly temperament so that you have confidence in it, not only when you are on its back, but in all your dealings with it. The only way for you to establish a happy partnership with your pony is for the two of you to have confidence in one another. This won't be possible if your pony is too excitable, or difficult a ride for your stage of riding. Remember, riding develops in stages. Your pony should be one you enjoy riding *now*; not one you hope to be able to manage next year!

Whatever kind, size, age or breed of pony you buy, it should be sound. This means that a veterinary surgeon should examine it, and find nothing wrong with it, and give you a certificate stating this. Apart from that, what matters most is that you should like the pony and feel happy riding it. You probably think that you would like any pony. But there are degrees of liking. You and the pony are going to spend a lot of time together; there shouldn't be any 'ifs' or 'buts' about what you feel for it.

Ponies, like people, have very different temperaments: you should suit eachother. If you're excitable, quick tempered or nervous, you don't want a highly strung, excitable pony. The two of you will spoil each other, and undermine each other's confidence. You want a calm, sensible even-tempered pony. If you're calm and sensible yourself, even an excitable pony will become calm when you handle or ride it.

Your pony shouldn't be too young. Some parents have the idea that it is nice for a young pony and a child to grow up, and learn, together. This is not possible. Only an experienced rider can teach a young pony how to be ridden; only an experienced, mature pony can help a young rider to improve. Ponies are not fully mature till they are five. Yours should not be younger than that; but it can be very much older. Ponies that have been well looked after all their lives can work happily well into their twenties. A pony is not too old because it is over ten. It is only middle-aged, and is capable of being a good ride for years to come. It is probably less expensive than a younger one.

It's also important that your pony should 'know its job': that it should be a well-mannered ride, understanding how to obey its rider's wishes. For instance, when asked with seat and legs, it should go forward freely at walk, trot, and canter: it should slow down without resistance, and stand still without fussing. Ponies that have been well trained when they were young will have good riding manners. But ponies have to learn how to be ridden, just as we have to learn how to ride. Therefore, it isn't sensible to buy a young pony and hope to train it yourself, because training, or breaking, ponies can only be done properly by experienced, knowledgeable people. A well-behaved adult, even quite elderly, pony can always go on learning. You can 'school it on': that is, improve the way it goes. Or you can teach it to play gymkhana games; or, if you're interested, to jump better. But that's quite different from trying to teach a young one which knows nothing.

Training ponies really begins, or should begin, when they are foals. It is based on two things: gaining the foal's confidence; and then, with patience, kindness but firmness, teaching it discipline: what it may do, and what it may not. First, it has to learn to wear a foal slip or a halter, and be led; beside mother, and then independent of her. Then, it must learn to let itself be handled all over, and then brushed with a soft brush, and let its feet be lifted. Although it can be playful, it must not kick or nip. Titbits therefore are not the best ways of rewarding foals for good behaviour. What foals really appreciate is being

72

scratched! Withers, manes, and their little fat rumps. Ponies that have been sensibly handled from foalhood are usually easy pupils when it comes to lungeing and backing because they have grown up having confidence in humans, and therefore accepting their discipline. Foals are so charming it is easy to spoil them. But if you let them have their own way too much, later lessons will be much harder.

One way to find a suitable pony is through your riding school. Your instructor will have a good idea of the kind of pony that will suit your stage of riding. Riding schools have their reputations to consider and are most unlikely to try to sell you something unsuitable. Another way is to contact the District Commissioner or the Chief Instructor of your local Pony Club, because sooner or later all children grow out of their ponies and want to be sure that they go to good homes. You can also read the 'for sale' advertisements in the horsey magazines or your local papers. Unless your parents know a lot about ponies take a really knowledgeable grown up with you to see the pony for sale, and follow their advice. Naturally, you want to ride a pony before deciding. Always let the person selling it ride it first, partly because you want to see what it looks like, ridden; partly because if it isn't well-behaved, it's better they should be bucked off than you! Handle the pony, as well as ride it. See if it's friendly in the stable; if it will let you pick up its feet, and is easy to halter, and to bridle.

If you're specially keen on a particular breed of native pony, a good idea is to write to the Secretary of that Breed Society, and ask for names of studs, or people, who have ponies for sale (see Societies and useful addresses).

It isn't wise to buy at a public auction. It takes a very knowledgeable person to pick a good pony at a sale, and not be 'run up' to too high a price for it. Also, nowadays so many pathetic elderly ponies are sent to sales to be bought by the 'meat men' that you will want to buy them all out of pity. For that reason, if the time should come that you have to sell your pony, don't send it to a sale. It has given pleasure and willing service. You would not want the animal that has been your friend and companion to end its days packed into a lorry bound for the slaughterhouse or a boat to Europe, to be killed for meat. Unless you have the time and the money to keep them in happy retirement, ponies that are too old to work should be put down at home; or taken personally by an adult to the abattoir or slaughterhouse so that it is certain they are immediately and humanely put down; or if you live in hunting country, taken to the hunt kennels.

7 Pleasure riding, shows and gymkhanas

Riding in company

It is enjoyable to ride in company, or even with just one other person. But always, even if you're with people you know really well remember your riding manners which are essential for safety as well as enjoyment. Naturally, you will be proud of your pony; ride it, therefore, as well as you can, but resist any temptation to 'show off'. Sometimes, you may feel that you are a better rider than your companions; all the more reason not to throw your weight about, or to start egging the others on to do things of which neither they nor their ponies may be capable.

It is never good manners for one rider to dash past another at speed. Whenever you want to pass someone – maybe you feel you can't control your pony unless you do – give them warning. Say 'coming on your left' . . . or 'your right'. Consider the other rider, whose pony may be excitable, too; give them a chance to control it, or things may develop into an uncontrolled race. When you go through gates (which must always be closed behind you) don't ride away until the person coping with the gate has closed it, but don't stand all bunched up together. The best mannered pony can kick if pushed and jostled from behind. And even if it's your best friend who shut the gate, perhaps needing to dismount, always say 'thank you'!

Whoever is in front of the ride should always signal before going faster: to trot or to canter. Those behind may be having a nice cosy gossip: give them time to get their wits about them, and their ponies paying attention. The front rider should also signal when slowing down, particularly coming back from canter to trot, otherwise the result may be a sort of motorway pile-up. When riding on country tracks, you can ride two abreast; it's good for ponies not always to go one behind the other. To give their pupils experience, country riding schools often take them out for a hack. The instructor in charge will generally arrange the ride in a particular order: do stick to it. If you're

It is useful to be able to open a gate from your pony's back. To do this the pony must learn to stand quite still when you ask it to, and 'move away from your leg', so that you can push it close to the gate, for you to be able to reach the catch. If you can open and close a well-swung gate, it shows that your pony is obedient, and your 'aids' accurate.

asked to ride at the back, it usually means you're considered competent enough to keep an eye on the riders in front of you!

Riding on roads

On roads, even on seemingly quiet country ones, always ride in single file, on the left of the road, and on the verge if there is one. If a vehicle is coming up from behind, the rider at the back of the ride should call out 'Car . . . or lorry . . . coming!'. If it is coming from the front, the one in front gives the warning. Many drivers are considerate, slowing down and giving plenty of room when passing. If you can't spare a hand from the reins to give a 'thank you' salute, do smile at them!

When you are riding along a road, don't relax and gossip. Keep your mind on the job; your right (outside) leg specially firmly on the girth to hold the pony straight and in to the left, and keep its head straight. *Don't* turn its head in, away from the traffic; this makes it easier for the pony to swing its quarters out, into the road. You can trot along straight roads, where you can see a long way ahead, but never trot round corners; you never know what you may find 'round the bend'. If you have to cross a road, don't take chances. Wait till both directions are clear, then trot quickly across.

When turning or stopping give clear hand signals to vehicle drivers and your companions. You should read the Highway Code, the section on 'The road user in charge of animals'.

You will be much more visible to drivers if you wear a 'dayglo' riding overvest, in orange or yellow – many London riding schools equip their pupils with them for added safety in traffic. Never ride in the dark or dusk without stirrup lights and light or reflective clothes.

Riding on bridleways
Fortunately, there are bridleways open in many parts of the country. Remember, though, that people walk on bridleways. They will not have a very good opinion of riders if on a wet day you dash past them splattering them with mud. Slow down when passing people on foot. Watch out for dogs, which sometimes yap at horses' heels. Don't ride on paths signposted 'Footpath'; they are only for people on foot. You can study a map of local bridleways at a Council Office, and they are marked on many Ordnance Survey maps.

If you have a friend with a pony the nicest thing you can do, if you live in suitable country, is to go off for the day together with a picnic and a map. Better still, make a real trail ride and stay somewhere overnight; this needs careful planning beforehand. You need to find and book a place for you and the ponies to stay and be fed – the English Tourist Board would be helpful. If you prefer to go in a group, the Endurance Horse and Pony Society organizes non-competitive trail rides (see Societies and useful addresses).

This is a Norwegian Fjord Pony foal; already you can see the distinctive cream colouring, and the dark line in the centre of the mane.

Above: The greatest of friends.
Left: At this pony club event, the pony is keen to join in with the riders.

When I was fourteen, my best friend and I did a wonderful trail ride over the Scottish border hills, from her home beside the Tweed to a fishing inn called 'Tibbie Sheils', by St Mary's Loch. In our saddle bags we took pyjamas and toothbrushes but, optimistically, no change of clothes. About an hour's ride from the inn, we got caught in a violent thunderstorm. It wasn't the rain that worried us; it was the lightning. There are no trees on those border hills; we felt very conspicuous. If we galloped and the horses got hot, would they be more likely to attract the lightning than if we walked and they kept cool –? I've never found out the answer to that one; anyway, it was far too wet to worry. We speeded on, and arrived, ponies steaming, soaked to the skin. The stables were ready for the ponies: we rubbed them down, fed them, gave them hay, and then went dripping, into the landlady's lovely warm kitchen, hoping to steam ourselves dry. Not a bit of it. We were fitted out with an extraordinary assortment of much-too-large garments in which we gratefully staggered to an enormous meal. In the morning, our clothes were dry, we rode back a different way, and arrived home glowing with a sense of adventure.

Riding alone

It can be dull to go for a walk alone, but to ride alone is never dull, because you are with your pony. It is then that real companionship begins to develop; the feeling that each of you needs, and is dependent on, the other. If you always ride in company or at shows or competitions, it is easy to think of your pony simply as a means to an end – a convenient way of getting about, or winning prizes. Riding alone, you have the chance of getting to understand and appreciate its individual character. And your pony, without others to distract it, will become far more sensitive not only to your 'aids', but to you as a person and how you are feeling. You will also discover, perhaps to your surprise, that your pony has a good sense of direction, and a long memory. If you're ever uncertain of where 'home' lies, slacken the reins and let the pony tell you. If you go on a ride you haven't been on for some time, you may have forgotten some of the turnings. The

A nice Palomino pony. The rider is a member of the Pony Club, you can see her badge and tie. She is wearing formal riding clothes including spurs, which should only be worn by an experienced rider. The pony is wearing a Pelham, which should be ridden with two reins, not with 'joiners', as this rider is doing. You can see the snaffle and the curb rings quite clearly; each should have its own rein attached.

pony will remember. If it is a native or part-native one, it will probably have a sure instinct which tells it when ground is unsafe, probably too boggy, to cross. Don't force it. Turn round if necessary and go another way. Alone, you will see more of the wild life of the countryside; birds and animals will not be nearly so shy, because you are quiet.

If you are schooling your pony alone, do remember how easily it can pick up your mood. If you are concentrating, and are really interested in teaching it something, you will hold its concentration and interest. If you're thinking of something else and then get cross because the pony isn't paying attention, all that will happen is that the pony will get cross too and will not be pleasant or co-operative. Always stop schooling when things have been going well, and you and the pony are pleased with yourselves.

Going to shows

Even if you haven't a pony of your own, you may be able to take one to a show. Riding schools often take ponies to shows in their neighbourhood and let their best pupils ride them. If you've been having regular riding lessons, you may be asked to. Otherwise you could hire your favourite pony for the day. Don't worry if you haven't all the right clothes, and can't afford to buy them specially; you can probably borrow what you need. If you are not competing, go as a 'helper'. You'll learn a lot, and have more fun than just watching. To have fun competing your pony doesn't have to be either expensive or well bred.

At big shows, the classes for children's riding ponies are for registered Riding Ponies: the aristocrats of the pony world (see photograph page 86). But nearly all shows have classes for ordinary ponies in which turnout and behaviour are as important as good looks and long pedigrees. Many have classes for Mountain and Moorland ponies, shown both in-hand, and ridden; sometimes one for each breed; sometimes just two classes, for large, and small, breeds. Large breeds are: Connemara, Fell, Dales, Highland, Welsh Cob and New Forest; small: all the others. Usually these classes are for ponies registered with their Breed Society, which means that they have pedigrees. If you have a registered pony of any one of the native breeds there will be many classes you can enter, both ridden and in-hand. In some classes the winners qualify for the Mountain and Moorland Ridden Championship at Olympia, and that would be a thrill!

82

This rider, without her jacket, is going to play gymkhana games. She is leading her pony properly, with the reins over its head. Although she is holding the reins in her left hand, it is really best to put your left arm THROUGH the reins, when leading, as then there is no chance of your tripping over the ends. Remember when leading not to have your right hand too close to the bit, and don't pull the pony along, or turn and look at it and try to drag it! On the left is a two-horse trailer, in the centre a one-horse trailer. These are less expensive than a horsebox and can be towed by a medium-sized car.

It's rather more likely, however, that your pony is of no particular breed. Don't despair. There are lots of other sorts of classes, and the gymkhana games too.

Handy Pony

In Handy Pony classes, behaviour really does count for more than conformation because the ponies will be asked to do all sorts of peculiar things, depending on what the organizers of the show have thought up. They may have to stand while you open, go through, and close a gate; walk into, and out of, a trailer; back down a line of straw bales; go over an imitation bridge made of planks, jump a small but

A test of skill for pony and rider in the Handy Pony class at a show.

probably very odd looking jump. It must do all these strange things willingly and obediently. The best looking ponies may make a hash of everything and leave you at the top of the line.

Working Hunter Pony
Working Hunter Pony is rather more advanced. Not only does the pony have to be a good jumper, but you must be a competent rider. The ponies will be asked to jump a course of six fences, the height dependent on the height of the ponies. Only the ponies which succeed in jumping the course stay in for the conformation part of the class. Here, looks do count; but again, the best looking ponies may not have got round the jumps. If you feel that you and your pony are capable of entering one of these classes, do school your pony well beforehand, and make sure that it will jump away from home. Nothing is more shame-making than having to retire because your pony has refused the first jump three times!

Best Rider
Many shows, and gymkhanas, have Best Rider classes. In these, it is YOU who are being judged, not your pony. But be warned. The judges of these classes often like to make competitors change ponies before making their decisions. They want to see how you cope with a strange mount: whether it goes better, or worse, for you than it did for its own rider. These classes often have a 'Best Turned Out' section as well. So even if you don't finish in the line-up of best riders, if you're particularly neat and tidy, your pony beautifully groomed and your tack immaculate, you may win a rosette.

Ridden classes
In ridden classes, at the start all competitors go round the ring together, first at walk, then at trot and canter. Try not to get stuck behind another rider. Equally, do not ride beside another rider, because one of you will be 'masking' the other, so that the judge cannot see you. If you feel your pony is being cramped or boxed-in by the one in front, it is quite all right to pass a rider, but do so quickly and neatly, preferably not just in front of the judge as though you were trying to catch his eye! The steward will call the ponies in to line, in turn; watch out for his signal. Then, each pony will be called out to give an individual 'show'. Make this neat, and brief: work out and rehearse beforehand what you are going to do.

In this showing class, the judge is running her hand down the pony's forelegs to feel for splints, and to check the tendons. Your pony must let strangers handle it as calmly as this one is doing. This rider is also very nicely turned out. The string round her waist is keeping her number in place; you must not forget to wear your number when you go into the ring!

The judge wants to see that your pony is obedient, and will trot and canter on each rein, and halt nicely. If you have taught your pony to rein back, you can do two steps of reinback after your halt, and then walk on, and return to the line.

At some shows, ridden ponies will also, after their show, be 'stripped'; saddles taken off, stood squarely for the judge, and then walked and trotted just as they would do if shown in-hand. A friend can come into the ring to help with this. When you're standing in line waiting your turn to give your show, don't 'coffee-house' (chatter) with your neighbours! And don't wave to mum or dad or friends at the ringside! For your pony's sake, keep your mind on the job.

In-hand classes

If you're going to show your pony in-hand, teach it to lead well, and to stand well. Many nice ponies ruin their chances in competitions by being awkward to lead and fidgety when standing. At both walk and trot, the pony should lead freely, level with your shoulder, neither pulling back, nor dragging you forward. At trot, which the pony should do to your word of command, don't have too short a rein; you should be about a foot (30 cms) away from the pony's side, and do run fast enough to let the pony show itself.

This is what happens, showing in-hand. First, everyone comes in and walks round the ring, probably several times. Then, one by one, the ponies are called into line. When all are lined up, the judge asks each in turn, starting at the top end, to come out of the line and show themselves. You come forward, towards the judge, and then you ask the pony to stand foursquare, head up, preferably looking bright and alert. The judge will inspect the pony carefully, and then ask you to walk away, and, probably, to trot back. Walk away in a straight line; when you turn, turn yourself round the pony, not the pony round you. Trot back straight, trot past the judge, and return to your place in the line, from the back. Don't go in from the front and try to push your pony in backwards.

It is quite in order to show the pony in its normal bridle, or you can have a show headcollar, to which a bit can be attached. I am sure I don't have to tell you to say 'thank you' if you are given a rosette!

For showing in-hand, you can wear riding clothes, or neat trousers, and a jacket, anorak or waistcoat over a shirt or sweater, depending on the weather. Avoid garish colours – quiet 'country colours' are suitable. Unless your hair is very short and neat you should wear something on your head. A headscarf, or a cap of some kind. Please, *not* jeans, or 'beanie' hats! Be sure your shoes are comfortable for when you trot your pony out; you can wear gym shoes, or 'trainers'.

Jumping classes

At local shows there are classes for riders with varying amounts of experience, including beginners, with low jumps. Don't ask a pony to do more than he is comfortably capable of. Walk the course first and remember to warm up and have a few practice jumps (but not too many!). Clothes are the same as for ridden show classes.

Gymkhana games

Gymkhana games can be fun. It's co-operation between pony and rider, rather than speed alone, which will win. But gymkhana games are hard work for ponies; to do their best, they must be fit. As well as being able to go fast, they have to stop and start quickly and make fast turns; all of which are strenuous exercises. It isn't kind, at the start of the holidays, to take a fat, grass-fed pony out of the field and expect it to carry you through a morning or an afternoon of games. You must get it fit first. Exercise it regularly every day, first, at walk and trot, then with short canters; give it gradually increasing amounts of concentrate feeds, and keep it for at least part of every day off grass.

It's also a very good idea to practise some of the games, especially those where you have to take flags out of pots, or put them into it; or lead the pony while you run beside it in a sack; or have to pick up and carry strange things, like balloons, or sacks. There's a useful little book called *Mounted Games and Gymkhanas*, published by the British Horse Society, modestly priced. It tells you how to play most gymkhana games and would be a help if you and some friends wanted to organize a little gymkhana of your own.

A very important point to remember is that in any game where you have to lead your pony, don't turn round, look at the pony, and try to pull it along. If you run, not holding the reins too tight, the pony will run beside you. It's always worth practising this. Never let go of your reins, whatever you may have to do dismounted. Get in the habit of slipping your left arm through them, so that you have two free hands, but the pony is still attached to you! It is also useful to learn to vault on to your pony, and to be able to ride it safely without stirrups.

Don't watch the other competitors; concentrate on whatever game it is, and don't get too excited or your pony will get confused.

If it's a relay, do try to slow down before the changeover, and do hold the baton well out towards the next rider; a lot of time is wasted in bad changeovers! Practise bending round poles at home; first at walk, then trot, then at canter, concentrating on getting the pony bending to your seat and legs, rather than hauling it round by the reins.

You must always wear a hat, but for gymkhana games you don't need a jacket. They're pretty energetic, and you'll be more comfortable in a shirt and tie, or a sweater, or a sweat shirt. Make sure your footwear is comfortable for running in. (See page 51).

Grooming and preparation
Whether your pony lives in or out, you want to groom it very thoroughly every day, for several days beforehand. Energetic grooming will have a more lasting effect on your pony's coat and make it look glossier than if you wait till the day before and then wash the pony all over. If the pony is grey, you will have to wash parts of it, to get off stable or grass stains. Shampoo mane and tail the day before the show. If you have a stable, even if your pony normally lives out, it will save you time in the morning if you keep it in overnight. To keep its tail clean, after shampooing, drying and brushing out, you can put it in an old stocking before bandaging.

Native ponies shown in Mountain and Moorland classes should have manes and tails untrimmed and unplaited and heels untrimmed. If your pony's mane is rather straggly, or uneven, you can tactfully pull a little to even it out, but never trim, or 'even off', the end of the tail, or trim the feather.

If your pony is of no particular breed, or is very well-bred, you can plait both mane and tail – less easy than it sounds. Practise beforehand! You can also trim its heels, being careful to make each leg look the same; trim the long hairs round its muzzle, and tidy its ears. Don't go poking round inside the ears with scissors; the soft thick hair lining the ears is a necessary protection to stop dirt or dust or foreign bodies getting in. Simply hold the two sides of the ears together, and trim off any hair that may be sticking out.

Do get everything ready the night before. If your pony is going by box or trailer, lay out the things you want for travelling: leg bandages or protectors; tail bandage; a sweat rug if you have one; fill a haynet,

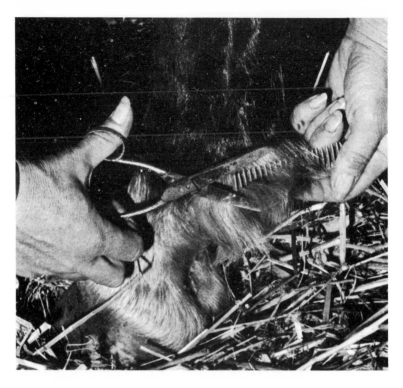

Trimming a pony's heels, using a comb and scissors. With the scissors, you clip off the hair protruding beyond the teeth of the comb. Only do this with mixed-breed ponies, never with pure Mountain and Moorlands.

and be sure you have a good clip-ended rope for the pony's head-collar. Make a list of everything you need to take with you, or you're sure to forget something. It doesn't sound possible, but I do know of someone who only discovered when she got to the showground that she had forgotten her SADDLE! 'You'll need your grooming kit, and hoof oil – be sure the tin is firmly fastened or it will leak over every-thing.' If your pony is plaited, take needle, thread and scissors (or rubber bands if you've plaited into them), in case plaits come undone on the journey. If the pony is grey, take a sponge and water brush to clean off travel stains.

If you're going to be away all day, take extra hay, so the pony has something to eat on the way home. Take a bucket for water; and one for the pony's feed at the end of the day, and the feed. If you have them, it's a good idea to take a spare girth and a spare pair of reins. When you set out for home, be sure you have everything with you! If you've had a picnic, collect your rubbish, and find a bin or take it with you.

On the day
When you are at a show, or a gymkhana, dismount at the end of your class, or between games. Don't be tempted to use your pony as a grandstand and sit on it all day. When you arrive, find out where riders are allowed to work their ponies in i.e. warm up and practise. There is usually a space set aside for this, separate from the collecting ring, into which you will be called about a quarter of an hour before your class. When you ride about a showground, do so at walk or trot only. Consider the spectators, who want to enjoy the show too, without constantly jumping out of the way of cantering ponies.

Competition is a good thing, if you think of it as a way of testing your skill, or your pony's looks and ability, against those of others. Taken to the extreme of 'win at any price', when the pony that doesn't win is sold and replaced by a 'better' one, it is not so good. It is far more satisfying to know that you have ridden your pony to the best of your own, and its, ability, than it is to win on one bought just for that purpose. Nor does money necessarily buy success; the most highly bred, expensive and well-schooled ponies will only win, even in the show ring where looks count, if they and their riders have formed a sympathetic partnership.

8 More about ponies

A very long time ago, in the centuries before Christ, an ancient race called the Celts lived in Central and Western Europe. They were a nomadic people: that is, they were travellers and wanderers, and they gradually settled in other parts of the world. Two tribes or branches of the Celts crossed the Channel and came to Britain, settling in parts of England, Wales, Ireland and Scotland.

Ponies were the only means of transport, so the Celts naturally brought many into Britain. But they also brought, among the gods and goddesses of their religion, a rather special goddess called 'Epona', who was the patroness of horses, asses and mules. It isn't hard to believe that our word 'pony' derives from that ancient Celtic goddess, particularly as no other language has a special word to describe small equines. All languages use the same word, with variations of spelling; in French it is 'le poney'; in German, 'das Pony'. Old sculptures and paintings of Epona usually show her seated with a horse or an ass beside her, her hand on its head.

Through the ages, ponies have been man's friends and helpers. Being amenable and adaptable, they have served him in many ways. In wild or mountainous countries they were, and in some places still are, the only means of transport, carrying both people and merchandise or household goods from place to place. When man has wished to settle, he has used ponies to help cultivate his land. Because they are tough and hardy, they have been able to subsist on whatever meagre rations could be spared them.

Ponies have been used extensively in war. Genghis Khan's Mongol warriors rode ponies. The Cossacks not only rode ponies, but often took mares and foals with them on their forays so that they could supplement their own diet by drinking milk from the mares. In Britain, in the 1st century AD, the Celtic Queen Boadicea drove three ponies harnessed to a chariot into battle against the Romans; there is a statue on the arch at Hyde Park Corner, London. In the Boer War, it was the skilled horsemanship of the Boers on their nimble, sure-footed ponies that held up and so nearly defeated the British. In World War I, Highland ponies were the mounts of the Scottish Territorial Regiment, the Lovat Scouts.

Ponies have provided sport and recreation. In India, polo was first played on small native ponies, many not more than 13.2 hh. For a long time after the British brought polo to western world, it was always played on ponies: the height limit was 14.2 hh. Nowadays, the term 'polo pony' is somewhat invidious, as there is no height limit. But almost certainly, ponies were cleverer at the game than horses. If you read a story by Kipling called *The Maltese Cat*, it will tell you just how much a clever pony can contribute to the winning of a game.

Long before there was official harness racing, or the highly-organized driving competitions of today, trotting races and trotting matches were the favourite recreations of country people in many parts of the world, using their native, working ponies.

Ponies have been used for adventure, sharing hardships and successes. The greatest hardship must surely have been that endured by the ponies taken on early Polar expeditions. The greatest and most successful adventure they have shared with man is the journey made by Mancha and Gato, two Criollo ponies, who were Tschiffely's companions on his 10,000 mile ride from Argentina to Washington. The ride lasted 2½ years and took the three adventurers over high mountains, through steamy jungles, and across waterless deserts. Mancha and Gato were already 15 and 16 years old when they set out; they reached journey's end fit, happy and in hard condition. Tschiffely took his two friends back to Buenos Aires by boat, and then went with them to a beautiful 'estancia' (cattle ranch) where he had arranged that they should spend the rest of their lives in freedom on the pampas. As well as '*Tschiffely's Ride*', which is the author's detailed account of the journey, Tschiffely wrote a charming book called '*A Tale of Two Horses*', in which Mancha and Gato tell their side of the story. The ride began on St George's Day 1925.

But if ponies could talk, I am sure they would tell us that it is with children that they have shared the most pleasure. Certainly there would seem to be an affinity between ponies and children, each enjoying the company of the other. Ponies can be extraordinarily patient with children's early experiments on their backs, and their often inexpert efforts at grooming them and putting on their tack.

With very young children, elderly ponies can behave rather like nursemaids, as though they were consciously trying both to look after and to teach their small charges! Even high-spirited ponies, with competent owners who like them to tittup about and show off, will usually carry a beginner or small child calmly and carefully. Where there is mutual trust, ponies are only too willing to co-operate in anything that's going, even if it means the indignity of being dressed up for fancy dress parades!

There is often more real companionship between a child and a pony than there is between many adult riders and their mounts. It is therefore a pity when ambitious parents, wanting to buy their children better ponies in order to win prizes, do not allow this companionship time to develop.

Whether or not we have a pony of our own, all of us who like them can do something to help ponies in general. Here are some of the things we can do.

1) There are several societies and associations and homes of rest whose aim is horse and pony welfare. But they are dependent on contributions from horse and pony lovers to keep going. By joining or helping in activities you will be giving help to many sad, ill-treated ponies and horses. If there is a home of rest near you, visit it. If you know how to handle ponies, you may be able to help in the stables. You may like to think up some ways of making money to donate, maybe a gymkhana, or sponsored ride. See Societies and useful addresses.

2) Not all stables, or places that hire out ponies for riding, are reputable, or well-run. If, perhaps on holiday, you go to a riding or trekking establishment where the ponies are in bad condition, apparently not getting enough to eat, or have sore backs or saddle or girth galls, your parents should report it. If the establishment shows a certificate or badge of approval, showing that it is approved, by the British Horse Society, the Ponies Association (UK) or Association of British Riding Schools, the report should go to the secretary of that body.

Even if it has none of these approvals, it should show a certificate saying that it holds a County Licence, in which case the report should go to the Council which is the licensing authority. If not, it is operating illegally, because anyone hiring out ponies or horses for riding is, in law, required to hold a County Licence. To get this, a veterinary surgeon has to inspect the condition of the animals and the tack, and the establishment has to carry third party insurance to safeguard its riders. Any establishment operating illegally should be reported to the local town or district authority. This may be a nuisance, but doing so will help both ponies, and riders. If broken tack, or other negligence cause an accident, it would be very hard to claim compensation if there were no insurance.

3) If in winter, you see ponies standing around in a bare field, looking cold and miserable, with nothing to eat and no water don't just say 'poor dears' and forget about them. On the other hand, don't rush off right away to find an RSPCA man, or a vet, because they *may* be about to be fed; their owner *may* be coming to feed and water them. Try to get a reliable adult who knows about ponies, to look at them, your riding teacher for example. If he or she agrees that the ponies are in need of care, it can be reported to the local RSPCA inspector. He may already know about them; if not, you will have done what you can.

4) Not all children who pester their parents into buying ponies know how to look after them – loving the pony isn't enough. If their parents are quite unhorsey, they won't be much help. If you've learnt something about pony care, you could be useful. Everyone who owns a pony likes talking to another pony person; without being too obviously curious, you could find out how it is being fed and cared for. If you're not bossy about it, you might suggest that perhaps the pony needs more (or less) hay, or grass; or a worm dose, or some concentrate food; or that its saddle doesn't fit, or its bit is uncomfortable. You could suggest lending a book about pony care.

5) You can very usefully spend time with ponies by offering to help with Riding for the Disabled. The disabled riders need an experienced adult, sometimes two, to help them with their actual riding. But someone has to lead the pony as well. If you can also help to get the ponies tacked up and ready, and untacked and fed afterwards, any Riding for the Disabled group will be glad to welcome you. If there is a group near your home and you own a

Riding for the Disabled. One person is needed to lead the pony and, depending on the child's disability, one or two to help it when in the saddle: one of these is always an experienced adult, often a physiotherapist. The pony must be absolutely reliable under all circumstances.

quiet, reliable pony you could offer to let it be used, yourself to lead it. Write to the secretary (see Societies and useful addresses) for a list of groups and information.

There has recently been a national championship for the best Riding for the Disabled pony, local shows running qualifying classes. The ponies have to be bomb-proof. They must stand absolutely still while disabled riders are lifted up, or climb awkwardly, on to them, and not mind if the rider's weight is not steady. They must walk calmly past all sorts of hazards; never shy or swerve, and lead well, halting, walking, occasionally trotting, calmly and obediently. As disabled riders vary in age and size from small children to adults, suitable ponies can be any breed, size, shape or colour. If yours turns out to be specially reliable, it might win an unexpected and worthwhile rosette.

Elderly ponies, too old for regular or fast work, can make excellent mounts for the disabled. Many groups would be glad to give one a permanent home, much better than sending it to a sale, or having it put down. A mare of my own worked happily till she was 29 with disabled riders in the South of England.

In the Brecon Beacons, Wales. Trekking enables you to go to places you might not otherwise see.

Societies and useful addresses

British Horse Society
British Equestrian Centre,
Stoneleigh, Kenilworth,
Warwickshire CV8 2LR
This is the official ruling body of
equestrian activities in Britain. It
holds progressive examinations
which are recognized qualifications
for riding teachers and stable
managers. Specialized committees
deal with the various riding
activities and horse matters.
Separate groups deal with
Dressage, Horse Trials, Combined
Driving, Long Distance Riding and
so on; competitors must register
their horses and be members of the
group and of the BHS.

Local committees around the
country deal with special matters,
an important one being the
establishment of bridleways and
rights of way. The promotion of
road safety is another. The
bookshop will send their catalogue.
The BHS book *Where to ride* lists
approved establishments.

British Show Jumping Association
The BSJA also operates from here.
All shows with show jumping
competitions offering more than £3
first prize money must be affiliated
to the BSJA; juniors and adults
entering affiliated competitions
must register their horses and be
members of the BSJA.

Pony Club This has its
headquarters here but affairs are
run by its own council.

The Welfare Committee
This is the special committee of the
BHS which deals with the
inspection and approval of riding
establishments. Complaints about
bad management or condition of
animals in stables should be sent to
the Secretary.

Horse Rangers Association
Mrs B. M. Gordon, The Royal
Mews, Hampton Court Palace,
East Molesey, Surrey

Riding for the Disabled Association
Miss C. Haynes, Avenue R,
National Agricultural Centre,
Stoneleigh, Kenilworth,
Warwickshire

*Association of British Riding
Schools*
Miss A. Lawton, Old Brewery
Yard, Penzance, Cornwall
TR18 2SL

Ponies Association (UK)
Mrs Margaret Mill, Chesham
House, 56 Green End Road,
Sawtry, Huntingdon, Cambs
PE17 5UY
This was founded by Mrs Glenda
Spooner, the Association's purpose

to promote interest in native ponies, encourage their breeding and that of good Riding Ponies; raise standards of pony care; and promote welfare. It runs three important breed shows: a spring Stallion Show in the South of England, a Scottish Show in July, and a Summer Show at Peterborough in August.

It inspects and approves riding schools, and riding holiday and trekking centres. Inspections are very thorough and unannounced; they are solely concerned with ride supervision and condition of animals and tack. Approved establishments are inserted in its *List of Approved Trekking and Riding Holiday Centres*, available by post.

National Pony Society
    Colonel A. R. Whent, Brook House, 25 High Street, Alton, Hants GU34 1AW
The various breed societies are responsible to this society for the accurate keeping of records and pedigrees; Riding Ponies are directly registered with it. It runs several important shows and organizes the Mountain and Moorland Ridden Championship at Olympia, London and a Mountain and Moorland Working Hunter Pony Championship, for which owners of competing ponies must be members of the society.

If offers two examinations recognized as career qualifications, for work with breeding stock, and with young ponies; students are eligible for grants and must train at a stud approved by the society. It organizes publicity and promotes interest abroad in British ponies.

British Show Pony Society
    Mrs J. Toynton, 124 Green End Road, Sawtry, Huntingdon
This society is for people who breed, own or show Riding Ponies. If you ever own a good registered Riding Pony, becoming a member will be useful.

Endurance Horse and Pony Society
    Mrs Paula Hancox, 15 Newport Drive, Alcester, Warwickshire B49 5BL
The EHPS organizes pleasure rides over interesting countryside, as well as competitive endurance and trail rides which are under veterinary supervision.

Breed societies
Secretaries of these will send information about studs breeding ponies, shows where they can best be seen, and people with ponies for sale. If you ever own a registered native breed pony, becoming a member will be useful.

Connemara Pony Breeders' Society
    Mrs McDermott, 73 Dalysfort Road, Salthill, Galway, Ireland

English Connemara Pony Society
    Mrs M. V. Newman, 2 The Leys, Salford, Chipping Norton, Oxon OX7 5FD

Dales Pony Society
    Miss P. A. Fitzgerald, 55 Cromwell Street, Walkley, Sheffield S6 3RN

Dartmoor Pony Society
    Mrs M. E. Danford, Fordans, 17 Clare Court, Newbiggen Street, Thaxted, Essex

Exmoor Pony Society
Mr D. Mansell, Glen Fern,
Waddicombe, Dulverton,
Somerset TA22 9RY

Fell Pony Society
Mr C. Richardson, 19 Dragley
Beck, Ulverston, Cumbria

Haflinger Society of Great Britain
Mrs H. Robbins, 13 Parkfield,
Pucklechurch, Bristol BS17 3NR

Highland Pony Society
Mr I. Brown, Beechwood, Elie,
Fife KY1 9DH

New Forest Pony Society
Miss D. MacNair, Beacon
Cottage, Burley, Ringwood,
Hampshire BH24 4EW

Norwegian Fjord Breed Society
Hon. Mrs J. Kidd, Maple Stud,
Ewhurst, Cranleigh, Surrey

Shetland Pony Stud Book Society
Mrs B. Macdonald, Pedigree
House, Kings Place, Perth

British Spotted Pony Society
Miss L. Marshall, 17 School
Lane, Dronfield, Sheffield
S18 6RY

Welsh Pony and Cob Society
T. E. Roberts Esq, 6 Chalybeate
Street, Aberystwyth, Dyfed,
Wales SY23 1HS

In case you are interested in a long-eared friend:

Donkey Breed Society
Mr D. J. Demus, Manor
Cottage, South Thoresby,
Nr Alford, Lincs LN13 0AS

Welfare societies and homes of rest
*International League for the
Protection of Horses*
67a Camden High Street,
London NW1 7JL
This does much good work
towards improving conditions at
sales, etc. and stopping live export
of horses to Europe for meat.

All homes of rest are charities and
are for horses, ponies and donkeys
suffering from ignorance, cruelty or
neglect, which are rehabilitated if
possible with people offering
satisfactory homes. Many animals
are young and can resume work
after veterinary care, rest and good
feeding. Homes welcome visitors –
phone first. Some of the best
known are:

Ada Cole Memorial Homes
Mr E. B. Collier (Director),
Broadlands, Broadley Common,
Nazeing, Waltham Abbey, Essex
EN9 2DH

Cherry Tree Farm, Newchapel,
Surrey

Little Church Farm, Wilstead,
Bedfordshire

Stepaside, Sandyford,
Co Dublin, Ireland

Bransby Home of Rest for Horses
Mr P. E. Hunt, Bransby,
Saxilby, Lincolnshire LN1 2PH

Horses and ponies in Middle Eastern countries frequently lead unhappy lives, particularly when old or injured. These are two very worthwhile welfare societies:

Greek Animal Welfare Fund
    Mrs Ware, 11 Lower Barn Road, Purley, Surrey
The fund is concerned with the welfare, care and rescue of all animals, but particularly with trying to find an alternative to the live export of horses to Italy for meat. A way to help is by sending your old Christmas cards.

Brooke Hospital for Animals, Cairo
    Mr R. Searight, British Columbia House, 1 Regent Street, London SW1Y 4PA
At the end of World War I some 20,000 Army horses which had served in Egypt and the Middle East were sold off locally instead of being brought home, the Army's excuse being lack of transport. Some officers of the Desert Mounted Corps took their own horses into the desert and shot them, knowing that otherwise they would work out their lives in appalling conditions, but many remained. In 1930 Major-General Geoffrey Brooke arrived in Cairo with his wife Dorothy, to command the Cavalry Brigade in Egypt, and Mrs Brooke was determined to rescue any of the abandoned warhorses she could find. Together they found many, all over 20, and bought those they could, stabling them locally for a few days' rest before painlessly ending their lives. Eventually Mrs Brooke raised funds for a permanent hospital, then called the War Horse Memorial Hospital. Mrs Glenda Spooner has written a book based on Mrs Brooke's diaries, *For love of horses.*
    Today it treats the sick and lame horses, mules and donkeys of poor and ignorant owners, for whom they are the only means of livelihood, teaching them that their animals will work better and live longer if well cared for.

Other addresses
English Tourist Board
    4 Grosvenor Gardens, London SW1
This publishes a booklet *Where to stay* which includes farmhouse accommodation.

English Riding Holidays and Trekking Association
    Homestead Farm, Charlton Musgrave, Wincanton, Somerset
This issues a list of riding establishments whose accommodation and animals are approved.

Irish Tourist Board
    150 New Bond Street, London W1Y 0AQ

The Horseman's Bookshop
    J. A. Allen & Co, 1 Lower Grosvenor Place, Buckingham Palace Road, London SW1W 0EL
This is the principal bookshop for every kind of horse book; their catalogue is available on request.

Glossary

aids means of communicating with and conveying instructions to pony. Natural aids: voice, hands, legs and seat; artificial aids, items of equipment.

Arab oldest recognized pure breed; all Thoroughbreds descend from it. Originated in Arabian peninsula.

bay dark brown, reddish or yellowish-ginger; black points.

black points black mane, tail and legs.

body brush oval brush held by strap, with tightly-packed small bristles, for mane and tail, and removing dust and scurf from coat.

breaking-in initial training of pony, now usually called schooling.

brown varying shades, body and points are same colour.

black uniform, white on head or legs possible; black muzzle.

cannon bone leg bone between knee or hock and fetlock.

chestnut ginger or reddish-brown, may be light, dark, or liver; lighter or darker mane and tail.

cob big-bodied, strong, short-legged pony or horse.

colt entire (i.e. not gelded) male horse under 4 years.

condition physical fitness and well-being.

conformation shape and build of pony.

curry comb tool with several rows of small teeth; metal, for cleaning body brush; rubber and plastic for coat.

dandy brush narrow brush with long stiff bristles for removing mud and dried sweat from coat.

dock bone of tail.

draghunt hunt where hounds follow a drag, an artificial scent.

dressage the performance of certain movements in a prescribed sequence.

dun various shades, all with eel stripe and often zebra markings.

farrier person who makes and fits horseshoes.

feather long hair on fetlocks and pasterns.

fetlock joint below cannon bone, above pastern.

filly female pony under 4 years.

foal pony under 1 year.

forehand part of pony in front of saddle.

forelock part of mane extending between ears over forehead.

frog V-shaped, shock-absorbing, horny part of sole.

gelding castrated male pony.

grey may be light, iron, fleabitten (i.e. with darker flecks) or dappled. Seemingly white ponies are termed 'light grey'.

gymkhana mounted competitive games usually for children under 16, many evolved from party games. Originated in India.

hacking riding for pleasure, going for a ride.

hand unit of height measurement, 4 in (10.16 cm), taken from withers. hh means hands high.

hogging cutting off mane with clippers.

in foal expecting a foal, pregnant.

in-hand led by bridle reins, head-collar or halter.

livery stable one taking ponies as boarders.

loose box a modern, self-contained, individual stabling unit with half-doors, pony loose inside.

lungeing training pony or rider on long line.

martingale tack item for controlling head position.

mare female pony over 4 years.

muck out clean stable, remove droppings and soiled bedding.

near side left-hand side.

numnah pad to go under saddle.

off side right-hand side.

Palomino golden; white mane and tail.

pastern slightly sloping part of leg below fetlock, above coronary band.

piebald coat with large irregular white and black patches.

pony animal up to 14.2 hh.

Riding Pony type developed from TB or Arab and native pony; has excellent conformation, elegance, with substance and pony character.

quarters, hindquarters part of pony behind saddle.

rump rounded part of back between hip joint and tail.

schooling training pony for purpose required.

skewbald coat with large irregular white and other-colour patches (excluding black).

skip container for collecting droppings.

stallion entire (i.e. not gelded) male horse over 4 years.

Thoroughbred, TB fastest, most valuable breed, usually has perfect conformation, descended from Arab.

water brush brush for washing feet and stains, and dampening mane and tail.

withers highest part of pony's back, at base of neck between shoulder blades.